LOOKING BACK

The Lighter Side of Olive Green Days

SK Kataria

Table of Contents

DEDICATION

This book is dedicated to all my course mates, seniors, juniors, and peers in uniform; who accompanied me on the reverie of my lifelong journey of 35 years in uniform. From the verdant landscapes of Dehradun to the vibrant environs of Chandimandir, each of you added vivid colours to the canvas of my life. Your camaraderie, quirks, and unwavering spirit have been the essence of these pages. This book is as much yours as it is mine, for without your interactions, anecdotes, and banter, these tales would have remained untold.

You all remain in my thoughts and loving memory, an inseparable part of this cherished journey.

PREFACE

Looking Back : The Lighter Side of Olive Green Days is not merely about revisiting the past but about cherishing the moments that defined the journey. Some might advocate always looking ahead, but looking back holds a unique charm - especially when memories are wrapped in camaraderie, laughter, and a sprinkle of whimsy. The grit and glory of life in olive greens often take centre stage, yet it is the unsung lighter moments that made the journey truly unforgettable. **After all, some journeys are too precious to only look forward.**

Spanning 35 years of service in the Army across diverse stations and tenures, these stories unfold from the gruelling days of military training to the challenging heights of Ladakh, and from instructional, staff, to command appointments. Each station added its own distinct flavour, balancing the rigours of duty with bonds of brotherhood and light-hearted moments that brightened the journey. This book is a tribute to those whimsical memories that sparked joy even in the most trying times.

Based on real incidents or anecdotes, the stories are infused with a touch of exaggeration to heighten the humour. While many tales are playful, a few delve into deeper reflections, proving that even laughter carries hidden lessons. Beneath the chuckles lie subtle insights that only time and experience can reveal.

Arranged chronologically along the journey's timeline, the stories also emerged spontaneously as they came to mind, a testament to how cherished memories surface without effort. The most heartwarming recollections often require no prompting; lingering on the fringes of thought, ready to bring a smile.

None of the stories are intended to cause discomfort. If the humour touches a nerve, it is purely coincidental and never meant to undermine anyone's dignity. This book is a celebration of shared laughter, the spirit of togetherness, and the enduring camaraderie that defines life in olive green.

While the book will resonate deeply with those who have worn the uniform or are still in uniform, it is equally meant to offer a glimpse to those who haven't - a window into the lighter moments behind the stoic exterior of military life. Beyond discipline and duty lies a world of warmth, wit, and lighter moments that give the journey its heart.

A distinctive feature of this book is the couplet at the end of each story, most of them self-composed. These couplets add a lyrical charm to each anecdote, binding together humour, emotions, and reflections in a few poignant lines.

This collection does not claim to be exhaustive but rather presents those stories that came rushing back, bringing smiles in their wake. As you leaf through these pages, I hope they spark a smile, or rekindle a fond memory that even the smallest moments of laughter leave the deepest imprints.

Looking back, the laughter shared and the bonds forged often outshine the hardships, proving that smiles outlive the years and memories march on long after the uniform is folded away. Prepare to be entertained, amused, and perhaps even inspired.

Brigadier SK Kataria (Retd)
kataria236@yahoo.com
April 2025

ABOUT THE AUTHOR

Brigadier SK Kataria is a senior Army veteran with 35 years of experience in combat engineering and infrastructure development. Born into a humble middle-class family, he was deeply influenced by his father, an educationalist, and his mother, whose dedication kept the family grounded. His Army journey began with clearing the Services Selection Board (SSB) interview while pursuing a Civil Engineering degree at Thapar Institute of Engineering and Technology, Patiala. Inspired by Army officers and stories of courage, he chose this challenging profession despite limited exposure to military life.

Graduating from Indian Military Academy (IMA) Dehradun was a defining moment. The gruelling training tested him, but his determination saw him through. Commissioned into the Corps of Engineers, he made a name for himself in Army courses, always a step ahead. He cracked the Defence Services Staff College (DSSC) entrance exam in his first attempt, becoming one of the youngest officers and the first in his batch to achieve this feat.

A proud Bengal Sapper, his career unfolded across a spectrum of instructional, staff, and command appointments. He served as an instructor at premier institutions like College of Military Engineering (CME) Pune and Army War College Mhow, proving to be a guiding light for future generations. On staff, he handled strategic roles, from Brigade HQ to the Engineer-in-Chief's (E-in-C's) Branch, where he led the charge on planning next-generation equipment for the Corps of Engineers, even taking on international assignments for procurement.

In command, he stood apart. Leading an Independent Engineer Squadron and later an Engineer Regiment, his units excelled under his leadership. He held coveted appointments across all spheres of the Corps of Engineers, a rare distinction for a senior officer. As Chief Engineer in the Border Roads Organisation (BRO), Military Engineering Service (MES), and the largest pivot Corps, and later as Centre Commandant of the Bengal Sappers, he steered his teams through challenging tasks while upholding tradition and operational excellence. Both his Regiment and the Centre earned Unit Citations during his stewardship - rare honours that marked his enduring legacy.

He has seen it all - deserts, high-altitude areas, obstacle-ridden terrain, valleys, and some of the toughest operational terrains in the world. From Sri Lanka with the Indian Peace Keeping Force (IPKF) to multiple engineer units, his career is a masterclass in leadership under pressure and an unyielding focus on teamwork.

Outside his professional life, he is a man of many interests. A keen golfer with a coveted 'Hole in One' to his credit, an amateur singer who can charm any gathering with retro Hindi tunes, and a passionate world traveller, he believes in living life to the fullest. Adding author to his list of achievements, he has already penned **'Life's Little Laughs : Delightful Tales from Our AWHO Society'**, a delightful book of stories inspired by community life. His current book **'Looking Back : The Lighter Side of Olive Green Days'** is based on a different theme alltogether, chronicling humorous and heartwarming moments from his Army journey.

His writings have found space in various newspapers like *Asian Connections*, where he brings out the lighter side of everyday experiences. He believes every phase of life has something unique to offer - the years in uniform were dedicated to duty, and now is the time to embrace new ventures with enthusiasm and curiosity.

He shares his journey with his wife, Sapna, a former educationalist turned homemaker, who's been his rock through thick and thin. Together, they've raised two daughters - one married and thriving, the other building a promising career after earning her MBA. Their family embodies resilience, harmony, and the joy of living.

<u>ACKNOWLEDGEMENTS</u>

No journey is ever truly walked alone, and this book would not have taken shape without the unwavering support of my family, who stood by me at every step.

My wife, **Sapna**, has been my steadfast companion not only in life but also in the making of this book. Her sharp memory helped me recollect many lighter moments, and she often suggested the punchlines around which some of the stories could be woven. Her knack for recalling impactful memories from the past helped me piece together scattered recollections into a cohesive narrative.

My elder daughter, **Tarunika**, planted the seed for this book after the release of my debut book *Life's Little Laughs: Delightful Tales from Our AWHO Society*. She felt that the lighter moments from my lifetime journey in uniform deserved to be chronicled. Her constant encouragement and warm appreciation of the initial couple of stories gave me the confidence to keep going.

My son-in-law, **Aditya**, added his touch of magic when I shared the first story with him. He appreciated the couplet I had enclosed with the story and suggested that adding a couplet at the end of each story would lend the book a unique flavour. His idea inspired me to embrace poetry as a fitting way to round off every tale.

My younger daughter, **Gunjan**, played a crucial role in giving this book its final shape. With her keen sense of design and sequencing, she helped arrange the stories in a smooth timeline, ensuring a consistent flow. Her creative touch in designing the front and back covers gave the book its striking first impression.

To my entire family, your unflinching support, thoughtful insights, and constant belief in my writing have been the bedrock of this journey. This book is a testament to most of our shared memories and laughter - a labour of love made possible by each one of you. I am deeply grateful to each of you for your invaluable contributions, encouragement, and belief in this endeavour.

<u>THE GREAT SWIMMING DEBACLE</u>

Joining the Army, if I may say, was a coincidence for me. As a civil engineering student, cracking the Services Selection Board (SSB) at Allahabad filled me with unparalleled delight. While my peers chased post-graduation degrees or some jobs, I basked in the glory of my selection. The aura of an Army officer, the crisp uniforms, and the disciplined demeanour - what could go wrong? I was convinced this was my calling.

But little did I know, life had surprises in store. I assumed that being an engineer, a coveted status in the civilian world; I'd be seated in a respectable office during training, sipping tea while others broke a sweat. Oh, how naïve I was!

Day - 1 at the Indian Military Academy (IMA) Dehradun, was memorable, to say the least. Reporting for documentation, I heard an announcement: "All Gentleman Cadets (GCs), report for a haircut!"

Having survived civil engineering of those good old days when it meant a real hard slog, I thought, how bad could this be? When my turn came, the barber gave me a sly grin and said, "GC, take one final look at your hair. Your head will never look the same again."

He wasn't kidding. The haircut? Zero from the sides and just enough on top to peek out of the beret. I stared at the mirror, thinking, Am I still me? The barber chuckled, "Welcome to the Army, Sir!" By the end of training, I couldn't imagine myself in any other style - it had grown on me, literally!

Classroom academics? No problem. Physical endurance tests? Manageable. Swimming? A NIGHTMARE.

As a Techo, I dreaded the pool. Unlike the ex-NDAs, who swam like dolphins, I resembled a confused otter. Weekly training programmes announcing swimming sessions gave me sleepless nights. My salvation came in the form of Ish Khurana, a fellow 'dreadful diver'. Together, we mastered the art of avoiding water. From lingering in the changing room to pretending to be unwell, we tried every excuse in the book. But Ustads have an uncanny ability to sniff out shammers.

One day, our Ustad gleefully announced: "Weak swimmers, report to the 10-meter jump board!" Our hearts sank. 10 meters? That's almost space travel!

Standing in line, Ish and I silently plotted ways to avoid climbing the ladder. But the Ustad's hawk eyes missed nothing. When my turn came, I crawled up the ladder at the speed of continental drift. At the top, the Ustad bellowed, "GC, walk to the edge and jump. You'll hit the water before you even know it!"

Easy for him to say. My legs felt like jelly. Summoning every ounce of courage, I stepped to the edge, looked down, and promptly wished I hadn't. Finally, with Ustad's coaxing, and my heart lodged firmly in my throat - I jumped. Instead of aiming for the pool's centre, I landed inches from the edge, nearly crashing onto solid ground.

The collective gasp from everyone around was deafening. They thought, some even muttered, "He's gone. Definitely broken a bone." Miraculously, I emerged unscathed, albeit drenched and humiliated. The Ustad's face was a mix of disbelief and exasperation. "GC, see your Platoon Commander in his office. Bajri-order!"

For three days, I endured relentless punishments - a small price to pay for surviving the 'JUMP OF DOOM.'

Today, when I think about that jump, I can't help but laugh. What seemed like a nightmare then is now one of my most cherished memories. Ish and I often joke about our legendary swimming skills and the hilarity of our shamming stunts. After all, the Army isn't just about discipline - it's also about the stories that make us laugh for a lifetime.

ख़ूब पर्दा है कि चिलमन से लगे बैठे हैं,
साफ़ छुपते भी नहीं सामने आते भी नहीं,
इक हौसले की ही तो कमी है वरना,
इश्क़ क़बूल करने को दिल मचलता ही नहीं।

<u>FRIENDSHIP THAT CARRIED THE LOAD</u>

Back in the days at the IMA Dehradun, I considered myself physically above average. Push-ups, chin-ups, 2-mile runs, 100-meter shuttles, monkey rope, vertical rope, fireman lift - you name it, I could ace them effortlessly. I even felt proud of my performance, often exceeding the set parameters for training. But mention the words '10-km endurance run', and my confidence would shatter into a million pieces.

The idea of running 10 km, especially with a full battle load weighing 22.5 kg, was enough to give me palpitations. And don't even get me started on swimming; you just finished reading about it! It haunted me for nights on end. It took every ounce of determination and a few retries in my third term, to finally pass the mandatory 50-meter swimming test.

But let me return to my arch-nemesis: the 10-km endurance run. This wasn't just a casual jog in the park; it was a gruelling affair that left even the fittest GCs gasping. As I reflect on it even now, the memory still sends shivers down my spine.

In the 2nd term, the endurance run began with a modest 5 km, but by the 3rd term, it escalated to the dreaded 10 km with the full battle load. The training was progressive, starting with runs in Physical Training (PT) rig and web belts, gradually increasing the load until we were running in full combat gear.

Every Saturday, I would anxiously await the weekly training programme, silently praying for no mention of swimming or endurance runs. But fate rarely listened. Swimming would inevitably pop up twice a week, and the dreaded endurance runs were always lurking around the corner. The night before these events, I'd find myself among a group of fellow 'weaker' GCs, huddling together and brainstorming far-fetched plans to escape the ordeal - most of which, of course, never worked.

During the runs, we passed through scenic tea gardens. Good runners revelled in the beauty of the surroundings, but for me and my fellow strugglers, it felt like a punishment. Running became a game of survival, with eyes half-closed and feet blindly following the rhythm of others.

One thing that made it bearable was the camaraderie. We ran in pairs or small groups, matching pace with buddies who shared our pain. This simple strategy turned agony into something more tolerable. Though I never enjoyed the scenic tea gardens like the good runners, I did find solace in the shared struggle. There was something reassuring about knowing I wasn't alone in my misery.

Then came the final test - the ultimate endurance run: 10 km with full battle load. It started before dawn, in the mild chill of the morning. We woke up at 3:30 am, going through the motions of gearing up, drawing Self Loading Rifles (SLRs), and cycling to the central fall-in point, all without any breakfast. By the time the long whistle signalled the start of the run, we were already low on energy level

The initial few km felt manageable. The cool air and adrenaline kept me going. But as we hit the halfway mark, fatigue started to creep in. At around the 5-km point, I stumbled on a stone and nearly fell. Though I managed to recover, something felt off. My legs felt heavier with every step, my breathing laboured, and my pace began to slow. Panic gripped me; the fear of failing loomed large.

That's when Arun Aggarwal, my practice buddy and one of the stronger runners, noticed me struggling. He slowed down to match my pace and asked if I was okay. I waved him off, telling him to go ahead and not let me hold him back. But Arun wasn't the kind to abandon a friend in need.

Without a word, he took my weapon from me, slinging it over his shoulder along with his own. "Keep running," he said firmly. "We are well within time."

His words were more than just encouragement - they were a lifeline. With his support, I pushed forward, one step at a time. Arun kept talking to me and reminding me of the finish line ahead. When I slowed, he'd nudge me forward, sometimes literally pushing me to keep moving.

The last few km felt like an eternity. About 500 meters from the finish line, Arun handed my SLR back to me, ensuring the Ustads wouldn't catch on to our little arrangement. "You're almost there," he said. "Don't give up now."

Somehow, I found the strength to cross the finish line. I passed the endurance test, but more importantly, I experienced a moment of camaraderie that stays with me forever. Arun had sacrificed his own time and ranking to ensure I made it through.

That's the essence of Army life - the unbreakable bond of brotherhood, the unspoken vow to never leave a comrade behind. Even decades later, I look back on that run not as a test of endurance but as a testament to the power of friendship. When my strength failed, it was Arun's unwavering support that carried me across the line - a lesson in resilience, camaraderie, and the extraordinary strength we draw from those around us.

तेरी उल्फ़त की मिसाल क्या दें हम,
अब तक कायल हैं वो क़िस्सा भूले नहीं हम,
तेरी हँसी की खनक अब भी दिल में है,
तेरी बातों की मिठास अब तक भूले नहीं हम।

THE DAY THE CARBINE FIRED
WITHOUT PERMISSION

Back in our time, the Corps of Engineers followed a peculiar tradition of allotting regiments to Young Officers (YOs) at the end of their YOs course at College of Military Engineering (CME) Pune. Though the groups - Bengal, Bombay or Madras Sappers were assigned at commissioning from the IMA, the exact regiments were announced later, shrouded in mystery and debates about fairness. While the Military Secretary's (MS) Branch called it a 'fair process', we YOs had our own theories, often attributing it to the whims of senior officers.

The announcement day was a rollercoaster of emotions. Those getting specialist engineer regiments - the so-called 'elite' units - celebrated, knowing they'd stay in peace stations. Others checked the location of their engineer regiments, hoping for a favourable posting. When my name came up, I was thrilled to be allotted the senior-most Bengal Sappers regiment. It was legendary, steeped in history, and celebrated for its honours. But my excitement turned into anxiety when I learnt the unit was deployed in Sri Lanka as part of the Indian Peace Keeping Force (IPKF).

"Kats, you're doomed!" joked my course mates. "Poor guy, you'll be a martyr in no time!" Their laughter didn't help my sinking feeling, but I soon reframed it as an opportunity. What better way to start my career than in active operations?

After the YOs course, a brief leave, and a heavy heart, I landed at Palali, Sri Lanka in January 1989. The Regiment Headquarters (HQ) gave me a hearty welcome - Army style - and I was soon despatched to Jaffna. The place was a war zone, with bullet-riddled buildings, daily reports of encounters with the Liberation Tigers of Tamil Eelam (LTTE), and the ever-present threat of Improvised Explosive Devices (IEDs) that kept everyone on edge. Our field company occupied a small, lagoon-side area with perimeter posts and strict security drills. Our offices and living accommodations were inside a desolate rest house.

Our tasks included repairing and rehabilitating infrastructure. Movement was risky and regulated by the Road Opening Party (ROP). We travelled armed, ensuring we didn't flout road timings. Despite the grim atmosphere, a stroke of luck arrived when my YOs course mate, Shambhu Bhatt, joined our Company on a cross-attachment for operational exposure. I was thrilled to have a friend around, especially since our Company Commander was a by-the-book officer with little room for flexibility.

One evening, the Company Commander issued his orders: "Both of you go together from now on. Stick to the road-opening timings and ensure strict adherence to drills!"

The two of us set out early in the morning with our engineer party in a Willys Jeep, accompanied by a 3-ton vehicle. We completed our task for the day and returned before dusk. As per protocol, we formed up for the mandatory weapon inspection. The Company Subedar ordered firmly, "Khali Kar!" (Empty your weapons).

Our soldiers flawlessly executed the drill, removing their magazines, cocking their rifles, and pressing triggers. No shots fired - it was textbook perfection. Then it was our turn. The Subedar eyed us and repeated, "Officers, Khali Kar!"

Shambhu and I raised our carbines. The sound of cocking echoed followed by... a deafening burst of fire!

Chaos ensued. Soldiers hit the ground, thinking it was LTTE fire. Sentries sprang into action, going for stand-to and scanning for threats. Meanwhile, I stood frozen, staring at Shambhu, who sheepishly realized he had forgotten to remove his magazine before cocking his rifle and then pressing the trigger.

The Subedar turned red with fury. "Kya kiya, saab? (What did you do, Sir?) You've scared the hell out of everyone!"

We all waited for the Company Commander to appear for the routine all-okay report, which he did every day without fail. Minutes passed. Nothing. He didn't emerge.

Finally, the Company Subedar dashed into the rest house to brief him on the incident. Moments later, the Company Commander emerged, visibly irate. He delivered a sharp dressing-down about carelessness, emphasizing the danger of such mistakes.

Why he delayed coming out remained a mystery. Some said he was too startled to face the noise; others joked he was waiting for the LTTE to finish their imaginary ambush, and there were even rumours that he'd sent his runner to fetch his pistol before making his grand entrance. Shambhu and I, though mortified, couldn't help but smirk later at the irony of it all.

And thus, the legend of the 'rogue carbine' became a part of company folklore, with Shambhu's misfire often retold over drinks - with increasingly exaggerated endings, of course!

गफ़लत में वो कुछ ऐसा सितम ढा गया,
किसी का चैन ले गया और ख़ुद बेख़बर रहा!

OPERATION BARREL RETRIEVAL

It was like any other day in Jaffna, where I stayed anxious in my field company - not because of the operational scenario due to the ongoing tussle with the LTTE, but more because of my Company Commander, known as 'terror'.

It was perhaps March 1989 when I was getting ready in my tiny room inside the bullet-ridden Rest House, right opposite Jaffna Town Hall. The place looked like a Bollywood movie set - an almost-ruined structure with a ghostly silence hanging over it. The Rest House housed our company office, a separate room for the Company Commander, another for his living quarters, and one relatively bigger space serving as the Field Officers' Mess.

I was to accompany my team to Elephant Pass, about an hour and a half away, where our company was executing some Field Flush Latrine (FFL) task for an infantry battalion. It wasn't the most glamorous sapper task, but in the army, even digging a hole comes with orders. Our team, as per standard practice, carried their personal weapons - carbines with me and the Junior Commissioned Officer (JCO), and SLRs with the men, along with one Light Machine Gun (LMG) mounted atop the 3-ton vehicle, accompanied by its spare barrel for redundancy.

I travelled in a vintage Willys Jeep, which made such a racket while moving that it could easily alert the LTTE from a kilometer away! My boys rode in the 3-Ton Shaktiman, which, despite its name, had neither 'Shakti' (strength) nor 'Maan' (respect), as it was sarcastically known!

At 8 in the morning, once the ROP had cleared the road and declared it safe for convoys, we set off in our two vehicles, carrying a few stores for the task. The assignment was straightforward but time-sensitive, which meant urgency was always on our minds. I still vividly recall my Company Commander's words when I was leaving for my first on-site visit: "Prepare a Work Programme for the task in hand and show me once you get back."

A Work Programme - a detailed chart outlining the resources, equipment, time, and effort required - was his favourite way to keep me occupied while I supervised work at the site. It was also his sneaky way of adding an extra chapter to my précis study. Throughout the day, my boys toiled relentlessly, ensuring the day's work was completed with a top-notch finish. Before leaving the worksite, it was standard drill to account for all personnel, weapons, ammunition, and stores. The JCO in charge ensured this was religiously followed. As the sun dipped below the horizon, fully loaded with weapons and gear, we started our return journey.

Once back at our Company location, the team lined up outside the office area to give the all-okay report to the Company Subedar. First came the customary 'Khali Kar!' (Empty Weapon) drill. This was protocol to ensure no accidental discharges. And then, it happened.

The Company Subedar marched up to the Company Commander, saluted smartly, and, with a nervous tremor in his voice, said: "Sir, everything is okay... but... the spare barrel of the LMG was inadvertently left at the worksite."

If the heavens had cracked open that evening, it would have caused less of a stir than this single sentence. My Company Commander's face turned from OG to an ominous shade of red. If LTTE's IED couldn't shake him, this news did. His eyes darted to his watch. The ROP had wrapped up. The road was no longer safe. But in his true style, he wasn't about to let an LMG spare barrel become our unit's legacy of failure.

"Kataria, take my Jeep too. Go back and get that barrel. And listen, weapons loaded, fully charged!" he roared, his voice leaving no room for negotiation. I instructed the radio operator to grab ANPRC-25 Radio Set to keep my boss updated.

Two jeeps roared back onto the highway, kicking up dust like a scene from an action movie. The Willys Jeep, despite its wheezing protests, did its best to keep up.

As I drove, I could almost hear my Weapon Training (WT) instructor in IMA yelling, "Your weapon is like your limb, never part with it."

 Yet, here I was, driving like a maniac to correct a blunder that had already sealed my fate. And what about my poor Company Commander? Professionally brilliant, extremely stickler, but would his career go down the drain along with mine? I was so preoccupied with these terrifying thoughts that I nearly forgot to keep an eye out for potential threat of IEDs.

Reaching the site, I breathed a sigh of relief on spotting an infantry guy standing with the spare LMG barrel in his hand. He handed it over to us and, in his typical infantry soldier way, gave my boys a mouthful and a piece of unsolicited advice.

We zipped back at double speed. On the way I reported back to my Company Commander over the radio. Certainly he must have broken into a full Punjabi Bhangra in his 'black dangri'! As soon as I reached, I walked up to him, stood to attention, and reported: "Sir, we have retrieved the spare LMG barrel. I am very sorry for the slip-up."

He looked at me with a mix of relief and residual rage, as if he had just been pulled from a sinking ship at the last moment. I have my doubts he ever reported this incident to the Commanding Officer (CO).

I learnt an important lesson: "Never assume. Always verify." And I suppose my Company Commander realized that Kataria could drive faster than the LTTE could plant an IED!

भरी महफ़िल में ज़िक्र जब दिलरुबा का हुआ,
मुद्दतों पुराने अफ़साने याद आने लगे।

<u>THE ROGUE FLY AND THE BLACK DANGRI</u>

Starting my career as a freshly commissioned officer in the senior-most Bengal Sappers regiment, I was mentally prepared for militancy, engineer tasks, and the sacred trifecta of discipline, duty, and decorum. What I wasn't prepared for was my first tactical face-off - not with an enemy, but with... flies and their merry band of insects.

Deployed as part of the IPKF in Sri Lanka, I landed at Palali with the enthusiasm and anxiety of a student about to meet the strictest principal in history. Guess who? Not the CO or anyone else, but the one and only Company Commander.

Now, this wasn't just any Company Commander. His reputation had spread faster than a viral video on the internet. Words like 'terror', 'no-nonsense' and 'by-the-book' were generously thrown around. Officers offered me sympathetic glances, the kind you'd get if you were heading into the den of a well-dressed tiger.

The road to Jaffna was no less dramatic. Every bump felt like it could be an IED. My neck did more swivels than a bobble head - left, right, forward, backward - exactly as drilled into us at the IMA. By the time we arrived, my body was exhausted, but my neck muscles deserved a medal for resilience.

And there he was - the Company Commander. A smart Sikh officer radiating authority sharper than the creases on his 'black dangri', which was tucked meticulously into his polished DMS boots, cinched with a web belt, and crowned with a pistol holster.

His handshake was firm, his words firmer. "Welcome, Kataria. You're here to learn. Not as Company Second-in-Command (2IC), but as a Platoon Commander. Get that straight."

No "How was your journey?" or "Are you settling in fine?" Nope. Straight to business - like a modern no-frills budget airline.

What made him unforgettable wasn't just his leadership style but that iconic 'black dangri'. Rumour had it the pistol in his holster wasn't standard issue but a family heirloom, passed down like a sacred relic, or maybe just a good luck charm.

Life under his command was - let's say 'unique'. While other company officers enjoyed movie nights with films of all colours, I was busy mugging up précis and General Staff (GS) pamphlets like my life depended on it. Not by choice, but by order! Dinner felt like a viva exam, with sharp sum-ups by my Company Commander.

But the real comedy unfolded in the Field Officers' Mess.

The Company Commander had a zero tolerance policy for flies and insects. Yes, flies and insects - not the LTTE, not operational lapses - just flies. One single fly would trigger a disciplinary monologue that would make even someone like Shakespeare envious.

"I do not like flies in the Mess! Why is there always one around during my meals?"

The poor Mess Havaldar would stand stiff, sweat trickling down his temple. "Sir, I ensure the doors are closed, windows sealed all day, and I even wave a towel before you arrive. ... I don't know how ONE fly sneaks in!"

This wasn't an isolated event. It became a daily affair like the evening roll call, but with more dramatic pauses and a lot more shouting.

One fine day, driven by curiosity and sympathy, I asked the exhausted Mess Havaldar, "How come I never see any flies when I'm around, but the moment he steps in - there's one doing aerial stunts?"

The Mess Havaldar glanced around, leaned in conspiratorially as if about to reveal classified information, and whispered, "Sir, it's not me. It's that damn black dangri he wears. I swear that thing attracts flies like a magnet. Not me, not the mess - just the black dangri, he repeated!"

I laughed so hard I nearly fell off the chair, which was already one loose screw away from collapsing. The thought of the Company Commander, the very embodiment of principles and discipline, locked in an eternal battle with a fly was irony at its best.

Of course, I never shared this groundbreaking discovery with my first Company Commander. After all, in the grand chessboard of life, even the fiercest king can be checkmated... by a fly.

हवा से क्या शिकायत हो अगर चिराग़ बुझ जाए,
कभी-कभी रौशनी के दुश्मन छोटे जुगनू भी बन जाते हैं।

CURTAINS, COCKTAILS AND THE ART OF QUICK WIT

My induction into the senior-most Bengal Sapper regiment was nothing short of unforgettable. It began at the Regiment HQ in Palali, Sri Lanka, where the stage was set for a welcome steeped in tradition, wit and a fair share of chaos.

The ceremonies kicked off with a exhausting Battle Procedure Endurance Tests (BPET) that stretched over several days, pushing me to the brink and making me question every past indulgence. Adding to the initiation was a mandatory week-long stay with the men and daily dressing-down sessions by every senior officer. Before I could catch my breath, I was summoned for what I believed was an interview with the CO. As it turned out, it was the Technical Equipment Officer (TEO) masquerading as the CO - an old unit tradition.

The TEO, a seasoned customer who looked reasonably old, possessed a razor-sharp wit and a knack for turning mundane lessons into unforgettable experiences. During the mock interview, he casually revealed, "I'm not the CO. But while you're here, come to my office this evening. I'll teach you a few things about the unit administration."

That evening, I showed up promptly, eager to learn. Instead of a lecture, I was handed a pile of acquaintance rolls and put to work assisting with pay disbursement. By the end of the night, I had mastered the art of pay disbursement, avoiding common mistakes, and even reading a soldier's mood through casual conversation. The TEO had his own unique teaching methods, and they left a lasting impression.

Meanwhile, the Adjutant - a towering and intimidating Khalsa - ensured my welcome wasn't entirely about lessons. He had my 180-pounder tent strategically pitched near the generator set, with its exhaust pipe pointed directly at the entrance of my tent. By day, I was under his sharp scrutiny; by night, the deafening noise ensured little to no sleep. It was a classic Army-style induction!

Eventually, the regiment de-inducted to Meerut, shifting from operational tasks to peacetime unit routine. Married officers, including the TEO, were allotted temporary lodgings in Candeth Enclave, a cluster of modified vintage barracks. Until his family joined him, the TEO lived alone in his quarters, maintaining a routine that balanced meticulous work during the day with quiet rum-soaked evenings.

One evening, as the TEO enjoyed his solitude, dressed lightly to beat the oppressive summer heat, a neighbour's children caught sight of him through his un-curtained window. Their father, a CO from another unit of the station, was less than amused. The next morning, he called up our CO to complain: "It's inappropriate for my children to see your TEO drinking half-naked. At least ask him to buy and put up some curtains!"

The CO, stifling his amusement, passed the message down to his 2IC, who summoned the TEO. When confronted, the TEO, unfazed and ever-witty, replied, "Sir, if he doesn't want to see me drinking half-naked, why doesn't he draw his curtains instead?"

The 2IC burst out laughing, and within hours, the story spread through the regiment like wildfire, leaving everyone in hysterics.

From that day on, the TEO achieved legendary status - not for his administrative prowess but for his quick wit and ability to turn even a reprimand into a punch line. As for the aggrieved CO and his family? Rumour has it they invested in thicker curtains and never dared draw them back again!

मकान अपना शरबत-ए-शराब अपनी,
जब चाहूँ पियूँ इसे बे-हिसाब।
पर्दों में रहना नहीं फितरत मेरी,
खुला मिज़ाज है मेरा लाजवाब।

<u>A YOUNG OFFICER'S BAPTISM BY FIRE</u>

In September 1989, my Regiment, freshly de-inducted from Sri Lanka, arrived home with a bag full of memories - some glorious, some nightmarish, and a few bizarre. Among our proud war trophies were an LTTE flag (displayed upside-down in our Officers' Mess, as per military tradition, of course!) and a solid wooden chair, rumoured to have once cradled the posterior of none other than LTTE Chief Prabhakaran. This prized relic was promptly placed in our field company, reserved exclusively for our Company Commander.

After months of war and near misses, we youngsters were all set to unwind in Meerut. But fate and my Company Commander had other plans.

"Pack your bags. You're moving to the College of Combat, Mhow, with a platoon."

I struggled to keep a professional poker face. "Why me?" I wondered. "There are others in the unit too!"

Then, to soothe my ego, I convinced myself, "Ah, it must be because of my exemplary handling of tasks in the war zone. Clearly, I have impressed him!"

At that time, Mhow had a field platoon attached with the College of Combat (which later rebranded itself as Army War College, perhaps to sound more intimidating because apparently 'Combat' wasn't menacing enough!). With great enthusiasm, I landed in Mhow, armed with a Willys Jeep, a 1-ton, and 3-ton vehicles, along with a platoon of men. My Company Commander even showed up to ensure we had settled in, a reassuring gesture.

The job seemed straight forward: provide combat engineering support to the infantry battalion and an armoured squadron in their training demos to various courses of instruction. Simple enough, I thought.

But soon, the situation took an amusing turn. Our role in 'combat engineering support' unexpectedly expanded into full-fledged landscaping! We suddenly found ourselves planting trees around the newly constructed College building, shaping fairways, and maintaining the under-construction golf course.

 Still clinging to logic, I approached the College Administration (Adm) Wing staff officer. "Sir, we have limited manpower. Could some of the golf course tasks be shared?"

He looked at me as if I had just insulted his ancestors. "Not my problem! Get additional men from your regiment!"

Great. I was now leading a covert horticultural platoon under the noble guise of combat engineering. My reports and submissions to my boss were met with nothing more than bureaucratic shrugs.

Then, one fine day, I was summoned by the Military Advisor (MA) to the Commandant, a renowned sailor who had circumnavigated the globe aboard 'Trishna' yacht.

"Oh no," I thought, "The Adm Wing must have complained about my lacklustre gardening skills."

But the MA had an even bigger gem for me. "I want a concrete basketball court built in the sports arena. One month, and I'll show its location on my way back home this afternoon."

I hesitated before responding, keeping my voice measured, as my boss had advised. Since the MA was also from the Sappers, I thought he'd understand.

"Sir, my boys are combat engineers, and I don't have enough tradesmen for the job. Who knows better than you that civil engineering falls under Military Engineering Service (MES) domain. Maybe they could --"

"Don't try to teach me! If MES was to do it, why are you here?" he roared. "Get cracking!"

With the weight of the world on my shoulders, I sat down with my JCOs.

"Saab, why not take MES' help?" one suggested.

Brilliant! Off I went, pestering the Garrison Engineer (GE). With some effort, I procured the design of a cement concrete basketball court and proudly presented it to the MA, along with a rough estimate.

"You think you're smart? MES design and costing? Nonsense. The court will be built by your men, my way, with my solid design, and within the funds I have sanctioned. Period."

I left his office in stunned silence.

With no choice, I launched into construction mode. My life became a circus act - one foot on the basketball court, another on the golf course, and my mind permanently stationed in the Adm Wing and MA's office, juggling progress reports and daily dressings down.

Word of my extreme suffering reached my regiment, and soon, the Regiment 2IC arrived. An outstanding basketball player with a knack for blending English and Punjabi into a linguistic masterpiece, he spoke with deliberate clarity. As is often the case with Punjabis - "we think in Punjabi and speak in English". With him, it was delightfully obvious!

The next day, he stormed into the College Adm Wing and then into the MA's office. What transpired inside was a mystery, but the aftermath was clear.

The MA called me in, looking furious.

"So, you complained to your regiment? Big mistake! If that court isn't ready in one month, I'll make sure you eat grass. And one more thing - forget MES posting forever!"

I gulped. Just when I thought things couldn't get worse, a DO letter arrived from my CO: "I hope you are feeling much relieved after the visit of the 2IC..." followed by a whole lot about how my problems had been magically solved.

Solved?! My situation had only gotten worse! While the CO was under the impression that the 2IC had fixed everything, I was left scrambling under an even tighter deadline with an even angrier MA and Adm Wing breathing down my neck. It was then that I truly understood the paradox of 2ICs - they may be your saviours, but they also have a talent for turning battles into wars!

शोलों पे चल के आओ तो कोई बात बने,
ख़ामोश रह के क्या करोगे अफ़साना लिख के।

<u>TORCHLIGHT TALES AND CAR CHARADES</u>

In September 1989, after the whirlwind that was Sri Lanka, we landed in Meerut, craving a much-needed breather. The peace-time tenure was a godsend, and the bachelors of the regiment quickly started plotting their outings, games, and of course marriage proposals. "Three years of marital bliss in Meerut" was the new dream for the eligible bachelors. Life was looking up.

Enter our protagonist: a tall, dark, and dashing young Captain from Hyderabad. Wasting no time, he married an equally striking lady from the South and brought her to the unit. While she struggled with Hindi and Punjabi initially, the regiment had its own 'methods' to ensure quick learning.

But this story isn't about language barriers. It's about their ride through life, literally.

Motorbike Madness

The Captain, proud owner of a second-hand motorbike, made quite the sight. In the evenings, he rode with his wife perched behind him, arms firmly wrapped around his waist - a picture-perfect image of marital bliss on two wheels. That is, until one fateful evening.

We spotted his motorbike speeding towards the Officers' Mess, but something was... off. The headlight was dead. Instead, his wife was sitting behind him, holding a torch and flashing its beam forward over his shoulder. The scene was straight out of a comedy skit.

"Sir," one of us asked, trying to stifle laughter, "why not get the headlight fixed?"

"What's the point?" he replied with impassive confidence. "There's enough light on the road, and the torch is good enough to warn incoming vehicles."

We all erupted into laughter. This 'torchlight innovation' became the talk of the regiment, with everyone wondering if he'd patent the idea.

Ambassador Antics

But the Captain's antics didn't stop there. Tired of his second-hand motorbike, he decided to upgrade to a second-hand Ambassador car. Not just any car - this was his ticket to impress his wife, who came from a civil background. The Mechanical Transport Officer (MTO) was now rolling in style. At first, he drove himself, but soon, leveraging his position, he appointed a guy from his MT Section as his driver.

Picture this: the Captain, in uniform, lounging in the back seat with one arm casually draped over the seat, while his soldier chauffeur navigated Meerut's roads. It was a sight to behold, and one that soon caught the CO's attention.

The CO's office was strategically placed near a road that led to the unit lines. One day, he spotted a white Ambassador cruising past, driven by a soldier, with an officer relaxing in the back seat. Alarm bells went off.

"Is that the Engineer Brigade Commander on a surprise visit?" the CO thought, suddenly sitting up. He stayed on edge all day, only to learn the Commander hadn't visited. The next day, the same scene played out. And the next. By now, the CO was positively stressed, believing the Brigade Commander had adopted this route to spy on the unit.

Finally, he snapped, ordering his Adjutant, "Find out where the hell the Commander is going every day. Has he changed the route to his office through our unit?"

The Adjutant, barely containing his grin, replied, "Sir, that white Ambassador? It's not the Commander. That's our MTO's new car!"

The CO was momentarily relieved, then roared, "Tell that bugger to change his route. I've had enough stress for a lifetime."

And just like that, the Captain's adventures in vehicular innovation continued to fuel regimental humour. Whether it was a torchlight replacing a headlight or a second-hand Ambassador stirring up CO-level chaos, the man sure knew how to leave his mark!

हम करें बिनबत्ती दोपहिया या अंदाज-ए-खास से मरकब की सवारी,
परवाह नहीं तानों की हमें, दीदा-ए-हसद रखते हैं अक्सर,
ज़माने में बेशुमार शख़्स।

WHEN SIMPLICITY OUTSHINES STRATEGY AND AMBITION

During peacetime, life in a regiment revolves around training and unit administration. Everything hinges on these two aspects. Back in the early '90s, during my extended first tenure that equalled two, I found myself attending many Combat Engineering Training Camps (CETCs). These annual month-long training sessions were a mix of theoretical lessons and practical exercises in field engineering and bridging. The grand finale was always a full-fledged regimental exercise witnessed by the formation commander, a test of our operational readiness.

Despite the rigorous schedule, there was always time for adventure. Hunting trips in open jeeps with shotguns were a weekly ritual. Rabbits, black partridges - whatever luck favoured - would later transform into a delectable dinner in our Field Officers' Mess. The mess itself was nothing fancy, just an EPIP tent big enough to house us all. Breakfast was a solitary affair, lunch generally at site, but dinner was the real deal. That was when all officers, young and old, gathered for a meal, usually with a tot of rum or whisky in hand.

There was, however, an unspoken rule. When the CO wasn't around, the evening was lively - casual banter, inside jokes, and lively discussions about the day's happenings. But the moment the CO decided to grace us with his presence, the atmosphere shifted. Conversations became formal, jokes evaporated, and officers spoke in measured sentences.

The CO loved his voice, and once he started speaking, there was no stopping him. For those who enjoyed a drink, it was an evening wasted. For teetotallers like me, it was pure punishment - sitting in near sit-up mode, listening to a prolonged sermon before finally being allowed to eat.

One evening, after the drinks had started working their magic, the CO decided to test our ambitions. He looked at a senior youngster and asked, "Ya! What's your aim in service?"

Taken aback, the officer hesitated before responding, "Sir, I want to do M Tech. I like designing structures."

The CO's expression darkened. He firmly believed that M Tech aspirants eventually drifted towards the MES that he viewed with suspicion. He turned to the next officer, hoping for a more acceptable answer. "And you? What's your grand plan?"

This officer, slightly more prepared, answered confidently, "Sir, I want to do Defence Services Staff College (DSSC). I've seen staff college qualified officers rise in service."

The CO was pleased. His mood lifted as he launched into a detailed discourse on the benefits of DSSC, the right approach to preparing for it, and how one must start early. Meanwhile, we exchanged glances, suppressing our amusement. And then, he turned to the newest officer in the Mess - a young chap from Manipur, fresh from his YOs course. He had joined the regiment just a month before it moved to Purkazi for CETC. Medium statured, expressionless, and a good football player, he had been quietly sipping his drink, unaware that he was next in line.

The CO's voice boomed, "And you, the baby of the regiment? How do you see yourself growing in the Army?"

The officer blinked, steadied himself, and, with the honesty that only two drinks can bring, replied, "Sir, I don't know much. My brother says - while you are young, just eat, drink, and make merry."

Silence. The CO stared. A few of us bit our lips to keep from laughing. Then, after a moment, the CO sighed, "Dammit! It's okay what you said, but you need to have an aim. Come on, say something more!"

The YO, still unbothered and in no mood for pretence, said softly, "Sir, if you insist, I want to become a Company Commander."

Now, this was totally unexpected. Even the Regiment 2IC was intrigued. "Why only a Company Commander?"

The answer, when it came, was as innocent as it was hilarious. "Sir, I have noticed that all Company Commanders have been given independent jeeps. Youngsters like us just keep running around on our motorbikes."

After a split second, the Mess erupted. Laughter rolled across, breaking all barriers of rank and decorum. Even the CO, the self-appointed guardian of serious discussions, couldn't hold back a chuckle. The youngster, with his unfiltered logic, had unknowingly delivered the lesson of a lifetime - live in the present, don't overcomplicate life with grand ambitions, work hard and let things fall into place.

जहाँ तक पहुँचना है क़दम बढ़ते रहेंगे,
मुक़ाम की परवाह नहीं सफ़र से मोहब्बत है।

THE ADJUTANT AND THE JUNK MOMENT

Meerut was a dream posting, especially for us bachelors. Evenings were a perfect mix - tennis at the Officers' Mess, casual visits to married colleagues, and long, carefree bike rides. At the heart of all this fun was our bubbly, ever-enthusiastic colleague, who had a knack for making sure no one took life too seriously.

But, as they say, all good things come to an end. Orders came in - our unit was heading for a high altitude tenure in Ladakh. The CO picked me as the next Adjutant. Maybe it was because I mostly kept to myself and had a serious demeanour, unlike my fun-loving predecessor, who had turned the Adjutant's office into a lively hangout spot.

Taking over the 'hot seat' was an experience. Previously, the company commanders would lounge around in the Adjutant's office, sipping endless cups of tea and indulging in animated conversations about everything under the sun. My predecessor, true to his nature, ensured the supply of samosas, jalebis, and juicy gossip never ran dry.

I, on the other hand, was different. Tea was offered as a courtesy, but small talk? Not my style. Discussions were strictly professional. The regular visitors soon found the office completely transformed. Their carefree camaraderie had given way to a structured, no-nonsense environment. Predictably, murmurs began - "The new Adjutant is too stiff!"

What they didn't realize was that the CO had his own channels of information. If anyone thought he was unaware of unit affairs, they were mistaken. The Subedar Major (SM) was his eyes and ears, keeping him updated on everything - from work progress to the general mood among officers and men. So, when the murmurs reached the CO, he wasted no time in addressing them.

One day, he called me in. "I like the way you work - focused, professional, no unnecessary frills. Keep it up!" he said.

That was all I needed to hear. A silent pat on the back from the boss was worth a hundred cups of tea!

As our move to Ladakh approached, the unit buzzed with activity - packing stores, coordinating with the railway authorities, and arranging special military train. One afternoon, I received a call.

A deep, authoritative voice spoke, "Can I talk with your CO? It's about your unit's special military train."

I responded politely, "May I know who's calling, sir?"

"I am Colonel Jung, the Movement Control Officer (MCO) Meerut."

I didn't catch the name clearly. "Colonel... Junk?" I repeated, confused.

There was a moment of silence. Then, a booming laugh erupted from the other end.

"Right you are, partner! Everyone becomes junk at this age and service! But just for the record, it's Jung: J-U-N-G."

Realizing my blunder, I felt my face burn with embarrassment. Stammering an apology, I quickly connected him to the CO.

Later, the CO called me. He was barely able to contain his laughter. "Sit down," he said, shaking his head. "So, you've decided to rename senior officers now? The MCO is many years senior to me too, and he just narrated your little Junk episode!"

I felt embarrassed. But to my relief, he continued, "He took it in good humour, don't worry. Just be careful next time!"

That evening, the CO couldn't resist sharing the story with some other officers. The very people who had thought of me as a tight-lipped, serious Adjutant were now in splits.

"Who knew you had such a sense of humour?" someone chuckled.

I simply smiled. Some pats on the back come with words of appreciation. Others come wrapped in a joke. Either way, I wasn't complaining!

बाज़ीचा-ए-अत्फ़ाल है दुनिया मेरे आगे,
होता है शबो-रोज़ तमाशा मेरे आगे।

THE UNBELIEVABLE CIRCLE OF FATE

During my first three years with the regiment, I had experienced my fair share of firsts and challenging assignments. By then, a posting was inevitable. Where to? Only the great MS branch knew. The Army harbours many secrets, and apparently, my posting order was one of them.

One fine day in early 1992, the long-awaited posting order finally arrived. But in those good old days, youngsters weren't informed. The CO had the final say, like a benevolent king who could grant or deny the privilege of movement. I remained blissfully unaware, wondering why all my course mates had long departed for greener pastures while I was still stuck, diligently fixing inventories and marking boxes.

Amidst this suspense, the Annual Administrative (Adm) Inspection loomed large. The unit was in full battle mode - files were being organized, weapons checked, and every inch of the premises scrubbed to perfection. Mornings were spent running BPET or standing on the drill square, afternoons buried in bin cards at the unit stores, and evenings lost in endless documentation marathons. The firing range became our second home, as if we were unknowingly being prepped for an impending invasion.

One such evening, during a dinner-night rehearsal at the Officers' Mess, our dear Adjutant let something slip. "Oh, by the way, when are you moving to the Engineer Squadron? Quite the prize posting!"

My ears perked up. "What? When was this decided? And why am I hearing about it only now?"

The Adjutant shrugged. "Oh well, these things happen," he muttered, almost embarrassed by his own slip of tongue. Annoyed, I realized I had no one to blame but myself for expecting otherwise.

The very next day, my Field Company was at the firing range. The CO, ever the perfectionist, personally supervised the performance of all companies. After my 'detail' finished firing, we jogged up to the Company Commander, who held our performance cards like an invigilator ready to shatter dreams. I had done well.

 The CO, too examined each card himself, his scrutiny sharper than an auditor with a magnifying glass. He looked at my report and said, "Good job, keep it up!"

But my frustration had reached its peak. Seizing the moment, I cleared my throat and asked insistently, "Sir, I learnt yesterday that my posting order has been issued. They say it's good for my career. May I plan my move?"

The atmosphere, charged with the intensity at the 'small arms range', suddenly turned still and ominous.

The CO glared at me as if I had just asked for his personal weapon. His voice thundered, "Bloody chap! I'll give you a two-pointer report, and your entire career will go for a six! You aren't going anywhere, understood?"

I stood there, stunned and humiliated. The posting had been granted based on my good performance, and yet here I was shot down like an overconfident duck at a carnival game.

The Adm Inspection went off well, and the regiment received accolades. But for some reason, the CO continued to look at me as if I were a fugitive out on bail.

Now, the Army has a time-honoured tradition for officers who dare to question authority - send them on endless courses! If physical exhaustion doesn't break them, mental fatigue surely will. Within days, I was packed off to CME for a course.

But fate had other plans. Not only did I survive, but I topped the course! I returned to the regiment, expecting a pat on the back.

Instead, the CO called me to his office. "Well, you didn't let the regiment down," he admitted begrudgingly, before dropping the real bombshell. "The regiment is moving to Leh in a few months. You take over as the Adjutant."

Was this poetic justice for the Adjutant's loose tongue? Or was the CO still determined to keep me 'sorted' in his own way? I felt like a Bollywood hero who had just escaped a bear, only to land straight into a tiger's den.

Looking back, I see the grand scheme of fate at play. Becoming the Adjutant gave me invaluable experience, and moving with the regiment to Leh turned out to be the adventure of a lifetime. CME, in hindsight, was a stepping stone. Two years later, I finally got my long-awaited posting - this time as an Instructor in CME. And the same Independent Engineer Squadron I was once denied? I went on to command it seven years later!

Life, indeed, comes full circle. One may have personal desires, but destiny alone knows the right time and space, and measure in which to grant them. And when it does, the outcome is nothing short of fascinating!

मंज़िल मिलेगी भटक कर ही सही,
गुमराह तो वो हैं जो घर से निकले ही नहीं।

LETTERS, LOVE AND THE LEGENDARY IL-76

In the grand tapestry of life, fate sometimes seems to have a wicked sense of humour. Just as I got engaged to my wife, the Army decided it was the perfect time to transport me off to the icy heights of Leh in September 1992. Perhaps destiny thought, "Let's make this love story more... snow-covered."

Within a few months, we bid farewell to the warm comforts of Meerut, packing up lock, stock, and barrel, and landed in the barren beauty of Leh. Now, my CO, probably feeling charitable or maybe just entertained by my 'newly engaged' glow, relieved me from one of the busiest appointments of Adjutant after the regiment's move.

I suspect he thought, "Let the poor chap focus on his fiancée. After all, surviving Leh's cold is easier than surviving a fiancée's 'Why didn't you write?'"

I was posted as the 2IC in a field company, a rather relaxed role made even more relaxing by my Company Commander. This officer had a different personality, always carrying a sense of humour, dressed in a manner that gave him a relaxed, civilian-like charm, and was obsessed with stock markets.

The Courtship Period

Ah, the courtship period - a magical time filled with dreams, hope, and... logistical nightmares. My fiancée was from a completely civilian background. She had no clue about army life, and I had no clue how to explain to her why I hadn't called in weeks.

Enter the unsung hero of military romance: the Field Post Office (FPO). It wasn't just a postal service; it was the lifeline of emotions, hopes, and connections. While modern couples fret over delayed texts, we considered ourselves lucky if our letters received replies within three weeks. Writing a letter was an event - drafting it over two days, despatching it with the solemnity of a royal decree, waiting a week for it to reach her, then another three days for her reply, and finally the return journey. All in all, it took about three weeks. Imagine that in today's world - if a message isn't responded to within minutes, it could well lead to a breakup.

Every time I posted a letter, I'd begin the sacred ritual of 'Waiting for the Reply'. Days were counted, faces changed colours with anticipation, and even my expressions couldn't conceal my interior emotions.

The Legendary IL-76 and My 'Majestic' Letter

Our makeshift accommodation in Leh had a front-row view of the runway - a perfect spot to watch the mighty IL-76 aircraft land. This wasn't just any plane; it was a flying fortress capable of carrying everything from tanks to my precious letters.

Now, here's where my Company Commander's humour took flight - literally. One chilly morning, as we sipped tea in our glass-covered verandah, the IL-76 made its grand descent. My boss squinted at the massive aircraft and, with the wisdom of a seasoned officer, announced, "The way the IL-76 is moving slowly and majestically on the runway... I'm sure it's carrying your letter. Must be the weight of all that love!"

I burst out laughing. That word 'majestically' was the cherry on top. From that day on, every time the IL-76 lumbered down the runway, I imagined it struggling under the sheer emotional weight of my heartfelt prose.

The Curious Case of the Winter Wear

Winter crept in, as it does in Leh, all gradually. Though it was just October, well before the expected snowfall, I spotted my boss walking back from an evening stroll dressed head-to-toe in Extreme Climate Clothing (ECC) - white jacket, white trousers, snow boots, OG gloves, and the infamous OG balaclava that made him look like a cross between a snowman and an undercover commando on a secret mission.

Surprised, I called out, "Sir, why the full ECC today? It's not that cold yet!" Almost spontaneously, he replied, "The weather here is like the stock market - unpredictable. I anticipate snow... any time."

I laughed so hard I nearly slipped on the non-existent snow. His dedication to preparedness was admirable, but let's be honest - he looked like he'd lost his way to a polar expedition.

Epilogue of Memories and Flying Fortresses

Decades later, whenever I see an IL-76 flying overhead from my flat, I smile, imagining it groaning under the 'majestic weight' of someone's love letter. And when winter rolls in, and I spot someone in my Society overdressed like they're braving the Arctic, I remember my Company Commander ready to conquer snow that never arrived.

वक़्त गुज़र जाता है मगर यादें ठहर जाती हैं,
कुछ ख़त, कुछ हँसी, और कुछ बेवजह की बातें।

WHEN INNOVATION MET HIGH ALTITUDE REALITY

Fresh from a 40-day leave during which I got married, I returned to Leh as a young Captain, brimming with excitement to begin a new chapter with my wife. We were all set to head to Tangste, where my field company was located, but destiny had a different script in mind.

The moment I stepped into the regiment HQ, I was met with two surprises. My company had been relocated to Kargil, and I was now the Officiating Company Commander.

My honeymoon bliss evaporated instantly. With a heavy heart and steely resolve, I accepted the challenge and moved to Kargil after a brief settling-in ceremony for my wife. Any dreams of a quiet and idyllic start to married life were swiftly replaced by the grim realities of high-altitude command.

A few days later, the CO called me. "Plan a water supply scheme for Dalunag and coordinate with the regiment HQ. The Corps HQ wants it operational this season."

Dalunag was infamous - a snowbound post perched at over 16,000 feet, under constant enemy observation, and cut off for six months of the year. Supplies of water, rations, and ammunition had to be stealthily hauled up from its adm base in the valley under cover of darkness by the troops of Sikh Light Infantry Battalion.

After meticulous ground reconnaissance, my team proposed an ambitious plan: a pipeline that would draw water from the river in the valley to the post at the summit, supported by booster stations and storage tanks along the way. It was a brilliant concept, but executing it in such treacherous terrain was akin to launching a military campaign.

For extremely demanding five months, my men toiled like mountain goats. Pipes were hauled up sheer vertical cliffs, strapped securely to their backs, and fastened with ropes. Pumps and generator sets were dismantled, made man-portable, and carried in parts to their destinations. The terrain was so unforgiving that the use of mules was out of question - our soldiers had to rely solely on their strength and skill, often scaling treacherous rock faces like seasoned climbers. Every movement was executed under the cover of darkness and in absolute silence to avoid drawing enemy fire.

When the project was finally completed, the water supply scheme stood as a testament to combat engineering ingenuity and sheer human determination. However, the pumps consumed diesel at an alarming rate due to their low efficiency in such extreme conditions. That, though, was a problem for another day.

The day of the inauguration arrived. The General Officer Commanding (GOC) and senior officers assembled at the adm base. Soldiers stood in formation as the crankshaft was turned, and water began its uphill journey through the pipeline. Cheers erupted, war cries of both the Infantry Battalion and my Regiment filled the air, and the officers radiated pride.

The GOC approached the troops of the Battalion and said, "Engineers ne kamala kar diya. Aap logon ki raat ki pareshani ab khatam ho gayi." (Engineers have done an amazing job. Your nightly struggles are now over.)

Yet, the soldiers remained stoic. Sensing their mood, the GOC turned to an outspoken Non Commissioned Officer (NCO) and asked, "Beta, why don't you look happy?"

The NCO responded with deadpan candour, "Sirji, problem taan same hi hai. Pehle raat nu paani dhonde si, hun diesel dhona painda hai." (Sir, the problem remains the same. Earlier, we carried water at night; now carry diesel instead.)

For a moment, there was silence. Then laughter erupted among the officers, rippling through the gathering. The Sikh NCO had captured the stark reality of innovation in extreme conditions with disarming wit.

That day, amidst the applause and celebration, his remark stole the show. Life at Dalunag remained as challenging as ever, but at least now, I had a story worth retelling.

हम पे मुक़र्रर हैं रंज-ओ-ग़म फिर भी,
हम ज़िन्दा हैं यह कम नहीं कोई।

THE REGIMENTAL GUEST WHO ALMOST GOT ME FIRED

The Army thrives on camaraderie, but sometimes that very bond can put you in an impossible predicament. Hosting a fellow officer is a sacred regimental duty - except when that officer is also your student, and the rulebook strictly forbids it.

It was January 1994, and I had just joined the Faculty of Combat Engineering at CME Pune as an Instructor. Still under scrutiny during my three-month probation, my instructional skills, composure, and most crucially, integrity were being closely evaluated. Any misstep could send me packing.

One evening, as I returned home on Asal Uttar Road, the door burst open. A young officer and his wife stood there, flanked by a typical Army-style black box, two oversized suitcases, and an assortment of bags. The officer beamed, "Sir, we haven't met before. I'm from your regiment, recently married, and here for a course in the Faculty of Combat Engineering."

I froze. I was the Course Officer for that very course! Housing a student was strictly prohibited to prevent conflict of interest. If word got out, my Pune tenure would be over before it even started.

I asked, "Why no prior intimation? And why bring your wife without securing accommodation first?"

With practiced nonchalance, he replied, "Sir, I did apply, but I doubt it reached the right desk. Since I was detailed for the course last minute, my seniors assured me - Kataria is there, so have no worries!"

Worries? I was drowning in them. My regimental instincts clashed with my survival instincts. My wife, ever the gracious host, welcomed them warmly, even asking, "Hope you get accommodation soon?"

That night, as we cleared the dinner table, I confided in her. "This is a disaster! If anyone finds out, I'll be reprimanded." She was unfazed and suggested, "They're here now. Find a solution instead of panicking." And so, a plan was hatched.

Over dinner, I told the officer, "You must not, under any circumstances, reveal that we know each other from the regiment. If anyone asks, let's just say fate placed us in the same Faculty."

He agreed, though he had no clue about the ticking time bomb he had dropped on my head.

The next morning, I took leave and dashed into the HQ, waving his prior accommodation request letter. After relentless persuasion and a touch of dramatization about his 'dire circumstances', I secured an allotment letter for temporary married quarters.

Triumphantly, I rushed home. "Congratulations! Your temporary accommodation is ready. You must move in today before someone else claims it!"

Sensing my urgency, they packed in record time. I even arranged a vehicle from the MT Section to ferry their luggage. Before they left, my wife handed them groceries and cooked meals.

As the vehicle rolled away, I collapsed onto the couch, exhaling for the first time in 24 hours. My career had survived barely.

To this day, the officer has no idea how close he came to getting me fired. Few in my regiment ever heard this tale. But that's Army life - when a brother officer lands at your doorstep, you step up. Even if it nearly costs you your career.

वो आफ़त बन के आए थे मेहमान बन के,
हमने चाहा निभाना पर जान पर बन आई!

THE VINTAGE CHARMER AND ITS LOYAL GUARDIAN

Back in January 1994, I joined CME Pune as an Instructor in the Faculty of Combat Engineering - a posting every Captain vied for. It was a pat on the back for enduring five long years of rigorous regimental life and excelling in courses. I arrived with my head held high, ready to impart wisdom. Or so I thought.

Initially, I was posted to the Field Engineering (FE) Wing, where I found two solid comrades. One was a tall, honest Major with a knack for clear-cut opinions and an inexplicable fondness for juniors over seniors. The other was a Sikh Captain, a man of remarkable communication skills and a great sense of humour. The three of us bonded instantly, our friendship sealed over endless cups of tea and crispy samosas during breaks.

Just when life was rolling along smoothly, fate decided I needed a challenge and shifted me to the Young Officers and Bridging (YAB) Wing. This was the equivalent of being thrown into a den of mischief-loving, unruly GCs. The schedule was punishing, the YOs barely trainable, and the patience required was Herculean. Despite the madness, our tea sessions continued unabated, if not daily, then at least once a week.

In those days, owning a car was a privilege reserved for senior officers. The rest of us made do with two-wheelers. My chocolate-brown LML Vespa was my pride and a trusty steed that never let me down.

Unlike us mere mortals, the Major owned a car - a turquoise-coloured Fiat Premier, acquired second-hand more than a decade ago, perhaps to impress his new bride. The car was, to put it politely, a relic. I suspected even its spare parts had gone extinct. But to him, it was not just a car. It was a legacy, a prized possession, a four-wheeled treasure.

Whether heading to the office, the shopping centre, or the Harkirat Singh Open Air Theatre, he drove it with an air of deep admiration that could make a Ferrari owner jealous. Every time it passed through CME, it drew attention - not for its elegance, but for the sheer miracle of its ongoing existence. Even cyclists occasionally managed to overtake it.

One day, in the spirit of friendship, we dared to suggest: "Sir, it's time to retire this vintage marvel. What if it breaks down in the middle of Pune? That wouldn't be a small embarrassment."

His reaction was immediate. His eyes darkened, and with an air of wounded pride, he declared: "I don't like unsolicited advice."

Message received. The Fiat was sacred.

One weekend, my wife and I decided to pay a surprise visit to the Major and his wife for an evening cup of tea. As we approached his house, we were greeted by an unforgettable sight - the Fiat in full surgical dissection.

All four doors flung open, the bonnet and boot raised, and in the middle of this spectacle stood the Major, in shorts and a T-shirt, scrubbing the car with the dedication of a man restoring a national monument. His wife, equally invested, was dusting the interior with meticulous precision.

"Welcome! Just give us a few minutes - we're almost done," he called out, beaming with enthusiasm.

"No hurry, sir. We'd rather enjoy the sight of this masterpiece," I replied, stepping closer.

That's when I noticed something strange. The window levers inside the car doors were missing. "Sir, how do you operate the windows?" I asked, suppressing a grin.

Without missing a beat, he responded, "Rear windows? No need to touch them - I've got them permanently fixed. As for the front, I generally keep them open for ventilation. No AC, after all. But when required, I have the levers in the dashboard to roll them up or down."

I stared at him. Then at the car. Then back at him. A true work of genius.

A few days later, we all went to the open air theatre for a movie. My wife and I arrived on our scooter, while the Major and his wife, true to form, arrived in their Fiat.

The movie was engaging, but once again, the Fiat dominated our chatter during the interval.

As we exited, out of sheer respect for the Major's unwavering loyalty to his car, we accompanied them to their vehicle. What unfolded next remains etched in my memory forever.

The Major approached the co-driver's side and pulled open the door extremely carefully. Unlike modern cars, where the doors swing outward from the back, this one swung open from the bonnet side. With a graceful nod, he signalled his wife to enter, much like a boyfriend escorting his date.

She stepped in, settled into the seat, and then - he banged the door shut with the force that would surely knock down a wall. But that wasn't the end.

With the ease of someone performing a well-practiced daily ritual, he walked over to the dickey, retrieved a nylon rope, and secured the door handle from the outside.

My wife and I stood there, frozen in disbelief. "Sir... what exactly is happening here?" I finally asked.

He looked at me, completely unfazed. "You see, the door latches are weak. Tried replacing them, but no spares available. This is my solution." And with that, he nodded, started the engine, and drove off at a speed that barely defied gravity.

We stood there, watching the majestic Fiat crawl away into the night, a moving tribute to its owner's devotion... and then, we burst into uncontrollable laughter.

What a man! What a car!! And what an obsession!!

इबादत कर रहे हैं तेरी एक मुद्दत से,
तेरे सिवा ना किसी और को खुदा जाना।

WHEN OMNI TRIED TO VANQUISH THE HILL

In June 1995, an unusual advertisement appeared on the notice board outside Harkirat Singh Open Air Theatre at CME Pune. It read, "Brand new Maruti Omni, just 500 km run, white, for sale." The name on it was of the Senior Instructor (SI), YAB Wing, Faculty of Combat Engineering. What made this particularly interesting was that the car was barely two months old, and the SI had been passionately raving about it since the day he bought it.

Back then, owning a car was a luxury. The Maruti 800 was the most sought-after private car among officers, admired for its sleek design, affordability, and reliability. It was a status symbol for senior officers and a dream for younger ones, who mostly zipped around on fancy two-wheelers. The Maruti Omni, on the other hand, was relatively new in the market. With its boxy design, spacious interior, and higher price tag, it appealed to a niche audience - larger families, pet owners, or those looking for something different.

This particular Omni came with an added feature that had everyone talking: an LPG-petrol dual setup. It could run on LPG for economical everyday driving and switch to petrol when extra power was required, making it a practical choice. After months of market surveys, test drives and deliberations, the SI had proudly made the Omni his own, parking it in the shed earmarked for him in the Faculty.

When the Omni first appeared in the shed, I, along with a few others, went to have a closer look. Its spotless white exterior gleamed in the sunlight, and its spacious interiors drew admiration. At first, we thought some visitor had mistakenly parked it in the SI's spot. But as we examined the car, the SI hurried out of his office and proudly announced it was his new buy.

The Omni quickly became a topic of discussion in the Wing. For the first week, the SI was often seen driving it around CME, his wife seated beside him and his children cheerfully perched in the back. He was visibly pleased with his purchase, and to celebrate, he hosted a tea party for the YAB Wing instructors. Over hot samosas, gulab jamuns, and tea, he shared his journey of choosing the Omni and why he believed it was the perfect car for his family.

But the real test for the Omni came when the SI decided to take his family on a weekend outing to Sinhagad Fort, some 40 km away from the CME. The trip began smoothly as the Omni buzzed confidently through Pune's bustling tabletop roads. But as they began ascending the Ghat section, the car started to show signs of struggle.

The Omni's pace slowed to a crawl. The steep incline seemed to sap its energy, and it barely managed to keep up. From the backseat, the children's voices grew louder.

"Papa, even the scooters are overtaking us!" they exclaimed in frustration.

"I'm doing everything I can!" snapped the SI, his grip tightening on the steering wheel as he toggled frantically between LPG and petrol, urging the wheezing van forward, as if sheer willpower could summon a burst of speed from its fading engine.

The Omni crawled uphill, its engine groaning under the strain. Scooters zipped past effortlessly, leaving the family red-faced in embarrassment. By the time they reached Sinhagad Fort, the excitement for the outing had evaporated. The children sulked, and his wife remained silent. After a brief and lacklustre visit, they decided to return to CME.

The SI's enthusiasm for the Omni visibly waned over the next few days. He seemed pensive, his usual cheer replaced with quiet contemplation. It was then that the advertisement appeared on the theatre notice board, much to the amusement of all.

The story of the Omni's uphill battle became a light-hearted topic of conversation in the Wing. Many felt that the ever-reliable Maruti 800 might have been a better choice. Some joked that the SI simply didn't know when to switch from LPG to petrol. Yet, the samosa party and the SI's candid recounting of his Sinhagad adventure softened the blow.

To this day, the tale of the Omni trying to vanquish the Sinhagad Ghats is remembered fondly - a reminder that not all well-planned decisions go as expected. Sometimes, even the most practical of choices lead to unexpected adventures, and in the end, they become stories worth sharing.

हज़ारों ख़्वाहिशें ऐसी कि हर ख़्वाहिश पे दम निकले,
बहुत निकले मेरे अरमान लेकिन फिर भी कम निकले।

PERKS AND PERILS OF HAVING COURSE MATES

In the Army, there's friendship, and then there's the bond with course mates - a unique connection that transcends time, rank, and sometimes even the rules. No matter where life takes you, these comrades become your partners in mischief, your go-to problem solvers, and your harshest critics.

Between 1994 and 1996, I found myself posted as an Instructor at the Faculty of Combat Engineering at CME Pune, a prestigious position earned through my prior successes in various courses.

Already familiar with the basics after conducting a few YOs courses, I was now entrusted with advanced combat engineering courses as well, including Engineer Officers Combat Engineering Instructor (EOCEI) – an extremely hectic program that tested both the mind and body. It wasn't just about teaching; it was about preparing officers for some of the toughest engineering challenges, from handling large-scale bridging operations to executing complex field engineering tasks.

To my pleasant surprise, two of my YOs course mates were nominated for this very course. After years of being apart, I was now going to be their Course Officer. One was a short, wiry dynamo, fearless and always up for a challenge, no matter how big the opponent. The other was the guy - a natural charmer, always smiling, and with a personality that could have easily made him the leading star in a Bollywood movie.

The first day of the course unfolded as expected - a formal briefing on the course structure, the dos and don'ts, the adm details, and the expectations we had from the student officers. The tone was professional, and the atmosphere was focused, but that changed as soon as the tea break began.

As I, along with a few other Instructors, reached the Tea Room, I overheard their familiar banter. "This course is nothing but pure torture!" one muttered, half in jest. "Yeah, it's like our units sent us here just to punish us," the other chimed in.

I couldn't help but smile, but then, as if on cue, my small dynamo of a friend shouted, "Jab saiyyan bhaye kotwal, toh dar kahe ka!" (Why fear when your beloved is the chief police officer?)

His voice rang out across the Tea Room, ensuring that every officer present caught his colourful commentary. Though the timing was perfect, I had to fight to hold back a laugh. It was one of those moments that could easily go awry in front of a group of student officers and the entire lot of Instructors.

I quickly composed myself and carried on, though the familiar dynamics between us were clear. Later that day, I called my enthusiastic friend into my office. With a grin, I said, "I love your energy, but let it not make my life harder than it already is. No more public wisdom like that please!"

He gave me a sheepish look, realizing the need for a bit of restraint. From then on, his outbursts were reserved for private moments. The handsome guy, on the other hand, knew exactly when to switch from charming to professional, maintaining the perfect balance.

The real fun, however, began during the practical exams. One of the first tests was the identification of bridging components - an exercise that required in-depth knowledge acquired through hands-on approach. As each student officer came in, the tension in the air was palpable. But when my short dynamo walked in, I knew this was going to be anything but a standard test.

While everyone else entered with a sense of discipline, he strolled in like he was walking into a café. He flopped into the chair with a dramatic sigh. "I'm not answering anything today," he declared. "I'm not prepared, and I don't intend to answer any questions. Let's just have a chat."

I could tell I wasn't going to ask any questions anyway, but I decided to roll with it. We spent the next 10 minutes reminiscing about old times, swapping stories, and having somewhat suppressed laughter. When he finally got up to leave, he did so with the same carefree smile, as though he had just aced the exam.

A few days later, the Medium Girder Bridge (MGB) written exam came up. As luck would have it, my charming friend showed up at my house, a couple of notebooks in hand. After a bit of casual conversation and coffee, he got straight to the point. "Buddy, I'm struggling with MGB design numericals. Mind helping me out? I promise I won't ask too many times."

I couldn't help but smile. He was clearly hinting at the fact that I had set the paper for the following day. So, as I helped him work through his doubts, I subtly slipped in a few key hints about the likely questions. It was a classic nudge-nudge, wink-wink moment, and he caught on quickly.

After all the exams were over, we met at the Officers' Institute. The Ha-Ha friend, visibly relieved, wrapped me in a hug and said, "Thanks, Kats." I smiled and whispered, "All your hard work, buddy."

My other ever-spirited friend then approached with a mysterious grin and said, "You have a knack for pulling me out of trouble. Can't thank you enough." I shot him a look and said, "You might have needed a hand, but you earned it. After all, you too are my course mate!"

The story of course mates is not just about what we learnt or the work we did together. It's about the moments, the laughter, and the shared experiences that stay with you long after the course ends.

दोस्ती का फ़र्ज़ निभाया यूं हमने,
कभी हँस के कभी हल्के से इशारा करके।

FROM WELLINGTON DREAMS TO BAREILLY JHUMKAS

During my tenure at CME Pune - a phase that polished my combat engineering skills and boosted my instructional prowess - life was rolling smoothly. The milestone moment arrived in 1996 when I cleared the DSSC entrance exam. The results came out in October and by April, I was all set to embrace the salubrious climate of Wellington. Like every officer fuelled by dreams of crisp Nilgiris air and cozy pullovers, I started preparing with enthusiasm, already imagining leisurely strolls amidst misty hills and a steaming cup of tea in hand.

But the Army, ever the master of suspense, had other plans. One fine day, while flipping through my books, I received an unexpected posting order. Not Wellington. Bareilly. I stared at the letter, half-expecting it to correct itself if I blinked hard enough. When that failed, I called the MS Branch - fondly known as 'Mysteries & Surprises' for exactly such plot twists.

"I believe there's been an error," I began diplomatically. "I was expecting Wellington, but this says Bareilly. A typo error, perhaps?"

The reply was swift, wrapped in Army logic. "No typo. There's an important exercise coming up – Exercise With Troops (EWT). Due to a shortage of officers, you're required in Bareilly before heading to Wellington."

I broke the news to my wife, who processed it with the stoicism of an Army spouse... until Bollywood's timeless track "Jhumka Gira Re, Bareilly Ke Bazaar Mein" popped into my head. Suddenly, the disappointment felt oddly musical.

We packed up - lock, stock, toddler - and landed in Bareilly. The regiment was bustling with preparations for an exercise in Ramnagar. A company commander, spotting me in the midst of the chaos, joked, "Look, a visitor has arrived!" Ah, the sweet camaraderie of Army humour - sarcasm served with a straight face.

Accommodation was another battlefront. No quarters for married officers were available. After much pleading, we secured a dilapidated, matchbox-sized flat meant for a lieutenant. Leaky ceilings, broken furniture, and walls so fragile you feared leaning against them. Notwithstanding, my wife's tears glistened with the silent strength of her inner courage.

The next day, I was to reach the Operations Room. The Design & Planning Officer (DPO) gave out the entire exercise plot, and then grinning like a man about to unleash a quiz, quipped, "Kats, fresh from clearing DSSC, give us some bright ideas for the exercise."

Mentally, I was still in Wellington, but I gathered my thoughts. "Sir, why not flip the engineer operation? Instead of moving South to North, let's go North to South. It'll be challenging, unexpected, and a true test of our operational fitness."

Silence. The kind that's loud enough to hear your own heartbeat - or in my case, the persistent drip from our leaky ceiling back home. After a while, the DPO cleared his throat. "Ah, interesting. But you see, changing it now involves logistics issues, clearances... you know the difficulties."

A chirpy company commander sitting beside me, whispered, "Some stage management is essential. We can't afford to fail the exercise."

And so, we did the exercise exactly as planned - predictable, smooth, and unsurprisingly successful! Everyone earned accolades, and not a single soul mentioned my revolutionary North-to-South idea.

After the exercise, we got a few days off. A bunch of us young officers decided to visit Tanakpur, cross the Sharda River barrage, and step into Nepal. Back then, crossing borders was as casual as crossing the street - a nod, a handshake, and the occasional 'friendly understanding' with customs.

In Nepal's Brahma Market, we shopped like diplomats on a budget spree - crystal showpieces and a grand carpet to cover cracks in the living room floor of my flat. We even hired a porter, loaded him like a festive mule, and crossed back into India with smug grins.

Eventually, my actual posting to Wellington arrived. As I packed again, the same company commander chuckled, "See? I told you - you were just a visitor!"

Looking back, he wasn't wrong. I arrived, shared unsolicited wisdom, attended an exercise, roamed around Nepal, and left - like an Army's own version of a plot twist. That's the beauty of Army life! You plan one thing, MS Branch plans another, and somewhere in between, life happens. And oh, what fun it is!

राह तकते रहे मंज़िल की,
मगर क़िस्मत ने रास्ते बदल दिए।

THE MYSTERIOUS POSTING ORDER

The DSSC exam was a battlefield - six months of sweat and toil, and if you survived, you marched through the golden gates of career progression. I had the good fortune of clearing it on my first attempt. Off I went to DSSC Wellington, one of the youngest officers on the course, allotted a top-floor flat in the farthest block on Gorkha Hills. My wife and our two-and-a-half-year-old daughter accompanied me, setting up home for what would be an intense yet unforgettable year.

The course was a relentless grind, but the friendships forged during those days were lifelong. As it neared its end, the biggest buzz was about postings. Who would receive staff appointments? Who would return to their units? Speculation fuelled every conversation - over coffee, lunch, and even candid exchanges between student officers' better halves. I was certain I'd be heading back to my parent regiment. It was generally the norm: junior officers returned to their units, while the more senior ones were slotted for staff roles.

Then came the much-awaited day. Posting orders were discreetly slipped into individual lockers at 'Chanakya'. As soon as word spread, officers scrambled to grab theirs like kids lunging for the last chocolate at a feast. I, however, strolled in with the calm confidence of a man whose fate was already sealed. Opening my locker, I found my posting order – '51 Engineer Regiment' - faint but unmistakable.

Days passed, and officers began receiving welcome calls and letters from their units. My locker, however, remained eerily silent. Finally, after two long weeks, a Demi Official (DO) letter arrived - but from the CO of 57 Engineer Regiment!

A chill ran down my spine. I yanked out my posting order and examined it like a detective on a high-stakes case. The old typewriter had played a cruel trick - what I had read as '1' was in fact '7'. My heart sank. My fate had been sealed by a fading ink ribbon.

Seeking clarification, I approached the MS Branch officer, hoping for a miracle. Instead, I got a curt response: "Where was the doubt?" He sent me a freshly printed, perfectly clear posting order - 57, not 51. Case closed.

So off I went to Sri Ganganagar, greeted with a grand welcome by my new unit. Being the only DSSC qualified officer, I was under constant scrutiny. My CO had high expectations, and soon, I was given a field company to command.

And my first assignment? Revamp the Officers' Mess. Before I could take a breath, another bombshell dropped - I was made Golf Secretary for 'Sudarshan Chakra Golf Course'.

The Deputy GOC, a Gurkha officer and a golf fanatic, called me over. I thought I might finally get a chance to learn golf at a young age. Instead, he fixed me with a piercing stare and declared, "The course is in shambles! Fix the landing areas, greens, gazebo, and add a walking plaza. And I want you here every evening."

My dreams of becoming the next Tiger Woods crumbled instantly. Instead of swinging clubs, I was landscaping greens.

Before I could wrap my head around my double responsibilities, my CO called me in. "Your company supports one brigade in operations. But since our division has four brigades and only three field companies, you'll have to take on an extra brigade's operational works too. Don't worry I will give you a few tradesmen pooled-in from other companies."

My face must have shown my exhaustion because he added with a grin, "I know you're overloaded, but remember - work is given to those who can handle it."

As I stepped out, a senior company commander, overhearing CO's remark, quipped, "No, work is given to those who don't know how to avoid it!"

I laughed, but deep down, I knew I was in for a rough ride.

My days became a relentless cycle - morning PT, a rushed breakfast, a hectic day in office, afternoons at the golf course, evenings planning the Officers' Mess revamp, and Sunday inspection of operational works at other stations - leaving my wife seeing little of me and my daughter barely remembering my face. Meanwhile, my fellow company commanders had mastered the art of 'strategic survival' - some conveniently developed chronic ailments, while others held late-night 'strategy meetings' to ensure they were 'too tired' for morning PT.

Yet, looking back, I wouldn't trade those two years for anything. They tested my limits, sharpened my skills, and proved that the toughest situations often shape the best professionals. Hard work never goes unnoticed. My CO never openly praised me, but I knew he was proud.

And in the end, one misunderstood digit on a posting order led me to a journey that built me...

जो मुश्किलों से भागे वो रास्ते में खो जाते हैं,
जो हंस कर चलें संग मंज़िल वही पाते हैं।

VIP NIGHTS AND THE SHY GURKHA'S GIFT

"You keep polishing this khukhri so regularly as if it is your most prized possession," my daughter quipped one lazy afternoon, watching me apply brasso with the precision of a jeweller working on his masterpiece.

Her observation was not new. This question had popped up several times before. But somehow, every time I tried to share its story, life would intervene - a doorbell ringing, a phone call, or simply the thought of pending chores. The khukhri's tale remained buried in my memories.

But that day, with no distractions in sight, I finally decided to spill the beans.

It was June 1998, when I had just reported to a new regiment at Sri Ganganagar as a Company Commander after completing my DSSC course at Wellington. The Infantry Division HQ had entrusted my regiment with the task of conducting the Annual Mine Laying Competition, a high-stakes event where the best mine laying parties (MLPs) from all infantry battalions would battle for glory. My field company was, in turn tasked to conduct this event by my CO, with some personnel provided from other companies as assistance.

For the uninitiated, laying mines is not just about digging and planting. It is a craft that demands precision, patience, and nerves of steel. The best soldiers from each battalion would be handpicked, trained for months, and sent to represent their units. The competition was the kind where the COs and Brigade Commanders would hover around like anxious parents at a school exam, hoping their battalion would walk away with the coveted trophy.

Our job as the conducting team was to set the rules, frame the questionnaire, and evaluate the mine laying drills. But something strange happened the moment the competition began - we became the most sought-after people in the entire Division.

Every night, as the MLPs sweated under the moonlit sky, food packets started arriving at our location. Not just any food - the best that battalions could conjure up. There were butter chicken parcels from one unit, mutton kebabs from another, and steaming hot jalebis from a third. Even the COs would discreetly whisper, "Do let us know if you have any preference for dinner tonight."

For one week, my team and I lived a life normally reserved for visiting dignitaries. We could not refuse anyone, not out of greed, but simply because saying no would send the wrong signals. And who in their right mind would refuse a hot meal served with so much affection?!

On one of those nights, it was the turn of a Gurkha battalion to take the test. The MLP commander was an officer who had done the staff course with me. A thorough professional, he was also painfully shy in my presence, addressing me in clipped, nervous sentences. His team performed with textbook precision - tapes perfectly aligned, mines laid with perfect drill, and timings spot on.

The morning after the final event, while I was compiling the results, a young Gurkha officer approached me carrying a neatly wrapped packet. "Sir, this khukhri is for you. Please do not say no."

I refused without a second thought. In the Army, gifts during competitions are strictly taboo - unless the gift is a cup of tea and some biscuits.

Later that afternoon, when the results were declared, the Gurkha battalion was crowned the winner. As the prize distribution ceremony wrapped up, the shy Gurkha officer finally mustered the courage to walk up to me.

"Sir, the khukhri was not for any favour, and as such the tests were all over. It is the way you and your team conducted the competition - so fair, so impartial... this is our way of showing respect."

His words caught me off guard. For a moment, I could not decide whether to feel proud or emotional. The man who had been avoiding eye contact all week now stood in front of me, eyes steady, offering the ultimate symbol of Gurkha tradition - the khukhri. I accepted it with grace, along with a box of sweets for my team.

That khukhri has been with me ever since. Its two miniature blades tucked alongside the main blade remind me not just of the Gurkha officer's sincerity but of those seven nights of unexpected VIP treatment - a once-in-a-lifetime moment when young Majors became the lords of the area, wined and dined by the very people who would not have batted an eyelid at us on any other day.

"So, you were a VIP for a week, in so quick time in your service?" my daughter asked mischievously. "Yes," I replied, giving the brass ring around the khukhri case a final, meticulous shine.

"Since then... I've stuck to polishing the khukhri myself - while my helper polishes the stars."

The sparkle in the khukhri matched the twinkle in her eyes, as if the blade itself had been waiting for its story to be told. It was not just a relic of a fleeting VIP week but a silent witness to values that stand the test of time - fairness, integrity and the respect they earn. The story had finally been shared, wrapped in nostalgia and polished with the same care that had kept both the khukhri and the memories shining bright through the years. Some stories age like fine wine, revealing their true essence only when the moment is just right.

नफ़े की बात हो तो फ़ुरसत ज़रूर है,
वरना ग़ैर दस्तयाब है ये वक़्त इस दौर-ए-बेरूखी में।

<u>FROM SENTINELS TO SINCERITY</u>

The beauty of our Army lies in its vibrant diversity. Infantry units are often composed of a single class of troops - Sikhs, Rajputs, Gurkhas, Nagas, Kumaonis, Marathas, and more - each with its own unique character. While Sikhs are known for their aggression and fun-loving nature, Kumaonis and Garhwalis exude simplicity, and Rajputs are the epitome of valour. Meanwhile, Mahar troops are known for their docility. But the officer cadre? It's a melting pot, where non-Sikhs might lead a Sikh unit, and Marathas might take command of Rajputs. Over time, officers adopt the quirks and ethos of their units, as do their families, creating a seamless camaraderie.

I recall one such experience during my younger days as a Major. Fresh out of DSSC and eager to prove my mettle, I was posted to a new engineer regiment. Though it shared the same mixed-class composition as my parent unit, the added responsibility of commanding a field company brought a unique blend of excitement and pressure.

The real adventure began when I was tasked to attend one operational discussion at Lalgarh Jattan where the Brigade HQ, that my field company was to support during operations was stationed. It was a small, sleepy town with a modest military station, but the Brigade Commander's Flag Staff House stood out - a grand bungalow with immaculately dressed sentries on guard. As a mid-level officer, I was acutely aware of the unspoken rules of these discussions: speak eloquently, but always align your 'best' option with the commander's preferred solution. It was an art I was learning on the job.

Among the COs present, the Mahar Regiment's CO stood out. He was a breath of fresh air, less eloquent in English, but his honesty and sense of humour were unmatched. His approach was like a compass - always pointing north, no matter the circumstances.

The operational discussions were intense, but the coffee breaks were where the real amity happened. Officers loosened, debating everything from global geopolitics to mundane unit affairs. By the third day, even personal anecdotes began to flow, and I felt at ease among this 'elite' group.

That evening, at the closing dinner, the mood was relaxed. With the operational discussions behind us, the talk turned to family. The Commander beamed with pride as he shared, "My son is about to complete IMA training and wants to join the Corps of Engineers." The COs collectively wished him luck, their admiration palpable. Another CO chimed in, sharing how his son, just starting at NDA, needed to bulk up to meet the rigours of service.

The Commander then turned to the Mahar CO. "You have a young son, don't you? Around 10? What does he want to be when he grows up?"

What followed was a gem of honesty that left us all in splits.

The Mahar CO, with his trademark sincerity, replied, "Sir, he's fascinated by the sentry at your Flag Staff House. He's captivated by the way he stands so upright, salutes sharply, and shouts 'Jai Hind Saab' at the top of his voice. Every time we pass by, he stops to stare at him. He tells us he wants to grow up to be that sentry."

A ripple of laughter spread through the group. With a grin, he continued, "I keep telling him, 'Aim higher. Be the person the sentry is guarding!' But he just won't listen."

The purity of the child's ambition struck a chord. It reminded me of a moment with my daughter not long ago. In a bustling market, surrounded by an array of dazzling and expensive toys, she fixated on a cheap plastic, but attractive Barbie doll. No amount of persuasion could sway her, and eventually, I gave in. Her innocent insistence reminded me of life's simpler joys - untainted by ambition or societal expectations.

As I sipped my drink that evening, I realized how much we adults could learn from children. In a world obsessed with climbing ladders and chasing titles, they remind us to find joy in the present, to value sincerity over status, and to see the world through an unfiltered lens of honesty.

The Mahar CO's son might never become the sentry he idolized, but his simple, heartfelt dream was a gentle reminder to all of us: sometimes, the beauty of life lies in its simplicity.

यह ग़ज़ब तो देखो मासूमियत की,
हम जिन्हें जन्नत की राह दिखाते रहे,
वो अपनी दिल्लगी को ही खुदा मान बैठे।

LICENCE TO FLAUNT : THE GREAT NAMEPLATE TAMASHA

The other day, during an evening walk in our pristine Society with my wife, we noticed an old, dusty Scorpio SUV parked conspicuously in the visitor's slot. Its rugged exterior was matched by its equally dishevelled middle-aged driver, standing beside it. But what truly caught our attention wasn't the vehicle or the man - it was the grand proclamation boldly displayed below the front number plate: "Astt Magistrate."

My wife, with her signature wit, said, "The age-old culture of flaunting designations still thrives in the civil world, while in the Army, it's almost extinct now!"

With a smile, I added, "True. Thanks to PM Modi, those red flashy beacons are history. Otherwise, every second car on the street, even one belonging to an ex-Sarpanch, used to parade a beacon with an appointment plate in bold, as if it were a badge of royalty and a status symbol. We Indians take immense pride in flaunting status, no matter how trivial it may be."

"Our Army wasn't untouched by this trend either," she quipped.

That topic dominated our conversation until the walk ended. After an early dinner, nostalgia crept in, and I found myself reminiscing about the 2K era when I reported to Beas for my first staff appointment in an Independent Mechanised Brigade - a coveted role for a Sapper officer, traditionally reserved for those from the Armoured Corps or Mechanised Infantry.

The Army, known for its distinctive style, had its own flair. Back then, you'd see gleaming staff cars and OG light vehicles polished to perfection, driven by sharply dressed, impeccably groomed drivers. An officer stepping out was always a treat to watch. His crisp uniform, shining brass on the shoulders, medal ribbons as fresh as morning dew, leather belt and shoes polished, topped with a smartly angled beret made civilians stop and stare. Senior officers added to this aura with Ambassador cars adorned with fluttering flags, star plates, Ray-Bans perched precisely, and sometimes even a swagger cane in hand. Make no mistake - officially, such grandeur was reserved for officers of flag rank.

Speaking of Army rides, their evolution itself tells a tale of changing times. From the rugged Willys Jeep till late '80s to the mighty Nissan Jonga, then transitioning to the sturdy Mahindra Jeep, followed by the sleek, agile Maruti Gypsy, and now the formidable Tata Safari taking the lead - it wasn't just about the vehicle but the aura it carried.

For commanding officers of major units, simplicity reigned. Against a bold red background, two brass letters gleamed proudly in front of their official vehicles: 'CO' - nothing more, nothing less. Crisp, clear, and commanding.

However, the trend outside the military painted a different picture. Even lower ranking civilian officers flaunted abbreviations like SDM (Sub Divisional Magistrate), BLO (Block Development Officer), and SDO (Sub Divisional Officer), often accompanied by beacons that could blind an owl. Even police inspectors had 'CO' on their jeeps - though for them, it stood for 'Circle Officer'. It seemed as if India had more VIPs than common citizens.

The temptation to 'keep up' soon crept into the Army ranks. Eventually, Army creativity took flight. Garrison Engineers

(GE), Officers Commanding of minor units (OC), and even Second-in-Command (2IC) found ways to sneak their designations onto nameplates. These additions were entirely unauthorized, and purely an exercise in ego.

One day at Brigade HQ, I spotted something revolutionary: a Gypsy boldly sporting 'COMMANDING OFFICER' across the front. It took me a moment to process. Not to be outdone, unit commanders of even the minor units proudly displayed 'OFFICER COMMANDING' on their vehicles.

But the pièce de résistance?

The HQ Company Commander, responsible for the Brigade HQ's adm needs, tried to affix a plate that read 'DEPUTY COMMANDER', in capital letters no less, emblazoned proudly as if the vehicle had been promoted. The irony? The Deputy Commander was a humble, down-to-earth officer who probably found this hilarious.

One morning, while sipping tea in my office with the BM - a towering six-footer whose breathing sometimes resembled a steam engine, we were joined by the HQ Company Commander. The conversation drifted to these pompous appointment plates for the vehicles.

The BM, with a mischievous glint in his eye, said, "Why don't I get my own appointment plate? After all, I'm the BM, the key staff officer here!"

Without missing a beat, the HQ Company Commander replied, "Of course! I'll have it fixed on your Gypsy tomorrow. And don't worry, I'll write it in full - 'BRIGADE MAJOR', for maximum effect!"

I couldn't resist joining the fun. "And what about my Gypsy? I'll need mine too," I said, maintaining a straight face.

The HQ Company Commander nodded thoughtfully. "Yes, sir! Shall I write 'DQ' for you?" I shook my head solemnly. "No, no. If we're going full throttle, write it in full - 'DEPUTY ASSISTANT ADJUTANT AND QUARTERMASTER GENERAL.'"

For a brief moment, they thought I was serious. Then realization dawned, and both burst into laughter.

"Sir, your appointment plate won't fit under the windshield we'll have to wrap it around the entire Gypsy!" they chimed in unison.

The hilarity of that moment stayed with us. At every gathering or mess party, when this story resurfaced, it had officers in splits. Eventually, higher HQ issued strict orders: no unauthorized appointment plates. Only Commanding Officers could display 'CO', and even that had to meet precise specifications for font, size, and placement.

By 2015, the government banned flashy beacons too. Common sense had finally prevailed. Yet, as my wife and I observed during our evening stroll, some egos refuse to retire gracefully.

हम को मालूम है जन्नत की हकीकत लेकिन,
दिल को बहलाने का ये ख़्याल अच्छा है।

THE BREATHLESS INTRODUCTION

Visits by senior officers in the Army are often viewed with the same enthusiasm as a surprise math test - necessary, but not exactly welcomed with open arms. They bring with them an avalanche of preparations: from polishing presentations and fine-tuning demonstrations to orchestrating grand lunches. In field areas, these visits are sharp and focused on operations. But in peace stations? Oh, they lean more towards adm finesse, where the biggest operation is ensuring the spoons in the mess are aligned perfectly.

After a whirlwind tenure in Sri Ganganagar, I found myself stepping into a coveted staff appointment in 2K of an Independent Mechanised Brigade. For an engineer officer like me, this was like getting front row seats to an exclusive show, a testament that I was doing well. But along with the excitement came the jitters. I had never served in a mechanised environment before, and now I had to prove I wasn't a square peg in a round hole. Thankfully, I'd heard that mechanised officers were large-hearted. Unlike infantry commanders, who could spot a misaligned button from a mile and lose their cool over it, these folks had an appetite for absorbing minor mishaps. Plus, they knew how to party, giving their young officers like me enough breathing space.

I landed in Beas, the humming HQ of the brigade and, coincidentally, the spiritual hub of the Radha Soami Dera. The Brigade Commander was a flamboyant Coorg officer with a heart of gold. His Deputy, in contrast, was as docile as a pigeon.

A few months into my new role, fully settled into the mechanised culture, we received the message that would set the entire Brigade HQ into frenzy.

"The new Corps Commander is visiting next week," declared the Brigade Commander during the morning conference, his voice dripping with both authority and the silent dread that such visits inspire. "Let's have a good show."

And just like that, the well-oiled army drill kicked into motion. The Deputy Commander, embracing his investigative instincts, dug up everything about the new Corps Commander. "Gentlemen," he announced in a separate meeting, "the GOC is particular about physical fitness. He has a unique sense of humour but won't hesitate to tick someone off. He's an infantry officer, so his actions will be loud and clear. Prepare accordingly."

The itinerary was crafted with the precision of a Swiss watch: introductions, briefings, a windshield tour of the station, and of course, a grand feast in the Officers' Mess.

On the D-day, we lined up impeccably turned out outside the Brigade Commander's office - Deputy Commander, the local station CO of our brigade, BM, me (the DAA & QMG), the Ground Liaison Officer (GLO), the Sparrow and other officers. Sequence was set, the nerves taut.

The GOC arrived, stepping out of his car with the swagger of someone who knew exactly how much power his handshake carried. He moved down the line, shaking hands, asking crisp questions, and nodding in approval. All was smooth until he reached the GLO.

Now, our GLO was a medium-statured officer with a belly that could be described as 'generously accommodating'. But he had a secret weapon - he could suck in his tummy with unmatched skill, giving the illusion of being as fit as the other officers. As the GOC shook his hand, the GLO activated his tummy-sucking superpower, drawing in his breath and holding it as if his life depended on it.

But the GOC wasn't one to be fooled easily. He kept shaking the GLO's hand, firing off question after question with the enthusiasm of an investigative journalist. One minute passed. Then another. The GLO's face started turning a shade of pink that even roses would envy. His eyes bulged slightly, pleading for mercy, but the GOC was relentless. Finally, like a steam engine releasing pent-up pressure, the GLO exhaled with a dramatic whoosh, and his belly jutted out.

The GOC, suppressing a smile, patted him on the back and said, "Ah, this is what I wanted to see, my friend. Impressive breath control! I'm sure the next time I visit; you won't need to hold it in."

I nearly burst into laughter, biting my lip to maintain decorum. The rest of the introductions wrapped up in record time - clearly, the GOC had achieved his entertainment quota for the day.

During lunch, however, the GLO was conspicuously absent; perhaps busy nursing both his bruised ego and his overstretched abs!

Such was the hilarity of the GOC's maiden visit - a day etched in memory, proving that sometimes, it's not the grand speeches or meticulous briefings that steal the show, but a simple breath... or the loss of it.

हम भी क़ामयाब होते अगर सांसों पर क़ाबू होता,
मगर पेट की साज़िश बड़ी शातिर निकली।

THE NIGHT OF THE FALLEN GIANTS

During Operation PARAKRAM, life revolved around preparing and waiting for the balloon to go up. As the DAA & QMG of an Independent Mechanised Brigade, I was neck-deep in work - managing logistics, coordinating moves, and ensuring supplies for the formation. Frequent relocations to deceive the enemy kept everyone on their toes.

Most movements happened at night, with tanks loaded on tank transporters; toed by massive Kolos Tatra 8x8 vehicles. The Engineers would lay temporary bridges across nallas, while permanent bridges were avoided to maintain operational secrecy. The drill was well set - entry funnels marked, load classification boards placed, and tanks offloaded from transporters before crossing the bridge.

One such night of March 2002, around midnight, a call came through, the kind that makes your heart skip a beat. "Sir... bridge collapse... One tank and transporter... both down in the nalla..."

I rushed to the site, expecting the worst. Fortunately, there were no casualties, except the pride of the Armoured and Engineer Squadron Commanders, who stood there looking as if they'd seen a ghost. The sight was bizarre - the bridge broken in the middle, the tank lying on its back like an overturned beetle, and the transporter resting beside it, as if offering company in misery.

The immediate question was, "How on earth did both go down together?"

Speculations flew faster than artillery shells. "Entry funnels must have not been made..." one officer whispered.

"No load classification board placed... how would the driver know if the tank was allowed to cross?" added another.

The most seasoned veteran JCO, who had been silently observing the chaos, muttered under his breath: "The bridge was fine... the funnel and load markings were all in place... the tank must not have been unloaded from the transporter...both went over together."

It made perfect sense. The standard drill dictated that tanks must be offloaded before crossing to avoid exceeding the bridge's capacity. But in the midnight haste, someone had taken the shortcut, sending both the transporter and tank together over the bridge. Midnight bravado had clearly trumped caution.

When confronted, the Armoured Squadron Commander mumbled something about saving time. The Engineer Squadron Commander, equally pale, probably wished the nalla would swallow him whole.

The recovery operation began the next morning, but the real punishment started that night itself. For the next month, the Engineer Squadron rechecked every bridge and culvert in the operational area - recce box in hand, pamphlets tucked under their arms, and heads bowed down. Meanwhile, the Sabre Squadron Commander became bridge-phobic, avoiding even the sturdiest of permanent bridges and sneaking across dry nallas like a smuggler. By the time the episode faded into routine, the standing joke in the Brigade was: "Sir, have we to cross over the bridge or bypass it?"

ख़ता करने में मज़ा है सज़ा पाने में क्या रखा है,
अगर नादानियां ना होतीं तो अफ़साने कहां होते?

THE OVERNIGHT BLOOM MYSTERY

Army life is full of camaraderie, competition, and the occasional bit of trickery. From 2003 to 2005, during my tenure commanding an Independent Engineer Squadron in Mamun Cantt, I encountered an unexpected rivalry - not in operations, but in gardening.

Upon arrival, I was fortunate to be allotted a beautiful house with a three-tiered front garden: the first level, a sprawling lawn the size of a tennis court; the second, a rose garden; and the third, a fruit orchard. A massive kitchen garden and a badminton court flanked the garden area. My wife, a passionate gardener, and I, an eager apprentice, set out to transform it into a paradise. With the help of a skilled gardener, we spent weekends and holidays planting, pruning, and perfecting every flower bed. Soon, our garden became the talk of the formation, drawing admiration from visitors.

With October came the challenge of planting winter flowers. Saplings of over 50 varieties were carefully planted, and as the months passed, the garden exploded into a spectacle of colours.

Just in time, the Formation Garden Competition was announced. Determined to present our work in its full glory, we labelled every flower bed and even placed a master board at the entrance to showcase our floral collection.

Next door, a CO from an armoured regiment in our formation and his wife were also enthusiastic gardeners - but their enthusiasm extended beyond their own lawn. Their Adm JCO frequently interacted with my Adm NCO, subtly prying for insights into our gardening techniques. Growing suspicious of their curiosity, my Adm NCO reported their peeping sessions over the fence. I simply laughed, telling him, "Let them watch. Hard work speaks for itself."

As competition day approached, my Adm NCO brimmed with confidence. "Sir, we are winning hands down!" he declared. But on the eve of the event, he rushed to my wife, breathless with urgency.

"Ma'am, something is very wrong! Till yesterday evening, some of their flower beds looked barren, their plants hadn't bloomed properly. But this morning, those very beds are full of lush, blooming flowers!"

My wife, ever composed, dismissed his concerns. "Relax. Focus on what we've built."

The jury arrived the next day, inspecting our neighbour's garden before heading to ours. My wife proudly walked them through the three-tiered masterpiece, explaining each plant and its seasonal bloom cycle. But one jury member, eyeing our display boards, remarked, "Ma'am, your neighbour has similar boards. Did your Adm NCO copy their idea?"

Indignant, my wife shot back, "Absolutely not! We create, not imitate."

The next morning, my Adm NCO, still on high alert, witnessed something astonishing - flower pots filled with blooming plants were being carefully dug out from our neighbour's flower beds! These pots, embedded into the barren beds night before the inspection, were now being discreetly loaded onto one ALS vehicle and driven back to their original home - the nursery. Their actual flower beds, which hadn't bloomed well, were once again exposed in their natural, bare state.

Ironically, our neighbour bagged First Prize, while we secured Second. My Adm NCO and our gardener, feeling cheated, looked to us. Smiling, my wife reassured them, "The truth has its own way of coming out. Hard work never goes unnoticed."

Sure enough, whispers of 'The Overnight Bloom Mystery' spread through the formation. What had started as a simple competition turned into an enduring joke - proof that in the Army, rivalry can bloom anywhere, even in the most unexpected gardens.

चिराग़ों की लौ तेज़ करने की ख़ातिर,
हवा दुश्मनी पर उतर आई है,
मगर रोशनी का मुक़द्दर तो देखो,
अंधेरों ने खुद ही शिकस्त खाई है।

THE ALLURE OF MAMUN BASHUP

It was the early months of 2004, a period of relative peace post Operation PARAKRAM, but for the army, peace is merely a canvas for wargames and operational discussions. The air was thick with preparation for a corps-level operational discussion on engineer support. I, fortunate enough to command an Independent Engineer Squadron affiliated to an Independent Armoured Brigade, was gearing up for my presentation at Ambala. Little did I know, the meticulously crafted presentation would soon be eclipsed by an unexpected 'operation' orchestrated by my boys back at Mamun.

The evening before the discussion, I cruised into Ambala in my hardtop Gypsy - a badge of command that came with pride and responsibility. My presentation was slated for the post-lunch session. Morning tea in the Operations Room had barely begun when an orderly burst in, urgency etched on his face.

"Sir, your Brigade Commander wants to speak with you. Immediately."

The tone was ominous. I quickly walked up to the other room, where the Commander's voice crackled over the line, dripping with barely-contained fury.

"Your boys have created some massive chaos here. Fall back today itself!" The line went dead.

My mind raced. What on earth had happened? I called my Squadron, but no one picked up. The air grew heavier with suspense. Moments later, the Corps Chief Engineer approached me, his face a picture of grim amusement.

"Your boys made national news. Apparently, they've beaten some civilians black and blue. I spoke to your Commander - he's livid. But before you leave, you're presenting first."

In 20 minutes, I delivered a presentation meticulously designed for 40. Nobody asked questions. Perhaps they all knew the real drama wasn't in the operations room but back in Mamun. With a hasty salute, I was out and racing down the highway.

By evening, I reached my Squadron. The story that unfolded was as bizarre as it was theatrical. One of my Troop Leaders, a fiercely loyal and hot-headed young officer, explained the situation.

"Sir, one of our boys, a simple, honest chap from Kerala, who is outliving with his family in Mamun village was cornered and thrashed by some villagers. They accused him of eve-teasing, which I'm sure he'd never do. When I heard this, I couldn't digest it. I took along a few guys and gave those villagers a lesson for life. A few might've ended up in the hospital."

"And the national news?" I asked, incredulous.

He smirked sheepishly. "The media got hold of a photo of an ALS truck. But it wasn't ours - it belonged to the armoured regiment in our Brigade. Their CO is probably having a meltdown."

I sighed, both exasperated and impressed. The young officer's honesty was commendable, but his methods? Questionable at best. I sent him off to cool down, knowing the real storm awaited me the next morning.

In my crisply ironed Number 1 OG uniform, I faced the Commander. His demeanour was surprisingly calm, though his words carried weight. Probably he had already been briefed about the complete episode.

"I've had complaints about villagers harassing our soldiers in the past too. But thrashing them isn't the solution. Your officer is young and dynamic, but he needs to mature. I'll handle the higher-ups."

Relief washed over me. However, the real comic tragedy was yet to come. The CO of the armoured regiment, whose ALS truck had starred on national TV, shuffled in after me, visibly drained.

"I'm getting hell for something my unit didn't even do," he groaned. "The Commander doesn't believe we weren't involved just because our ALS got caught on camera. He's called me in thrice already to 'confess.'"

I bit back a laugh, giving him my sympathetic look. In the army, guilt by association can be as damning as the act itself.

Later, I reflected on the absurdity of it all. An operational discussion overshadowed by a village skirmish, a young officer who turned vigilante, and a misattributed ALS vehicle that became the scapegoat of national headlines. Such are the theatrics of army life - where even the most meticulously planned manoeuvres can be derailed by the unpredictable chaos of human nature.

हम आह भी भरते हैं तो हो जाते हैं बदनाम,
वो क़त्ल भी करते हैं तो चर्चा नहीं होती।

DESTINY'S PRANK : A CO'S ROLLERCOASTER RIDE

It seemed as though fate had a wicked sense of humour when it came to my postings. Every new posting order brought a jolt of surprise, like expecting a warm cup of tea and being handed a cold glass of lassi instead. Having commanded an Independent Engineer Squadron, I eagerly awaited my next assignment in the newly promoted rank. Naturally, I assumed I would be returning to my parent regiment as its CO, especially since the incumbent was due for turnover. But, as always, destiny had other plans.

One fine morning in March 2005, I received my posting order. With the eagerness of a child unwrapping a long-anticipated gift, I tore it open. And there it was – an entirely different Engineer Regiment! A regiment I had never even remotely imagined commanding. It was as if the universe had decided to play a practical joke on me.

Dumbfounded, I immediately called up the Colonel Commandant's office. His staff officer, sensing my agitation, hesitated before asking, "Sir, you seem perturbed. May I inquire why?"

"My posting, of course," I retorted, my voice laced with incredulity.

The Colonel Commandant, an approachable yet formidable man, took my call. Without mincing words, I blurted out, "Sir, I think I'm being given step motherly treatment! Every regimental tenure of mine has been with a different unit. Why can't I command my parent regiment when it is falling vacant?"

He snickered something I wasn't expecting. "All regiments are alike, my dear Kataria. You should be happier for the exposure to different units. One day, you'll end up as the Centre Commandant!"

I knew he said so just to silence me from quizzing him further. That was the end of the call, just a cryptic prophecy that, at the time, sounded as random as a street astrologer's prediction.

With a resigned sigh, I packed my bags and headed to Leh, where my new regiment was stationed. It was a regiment of great repute, and I was determined to uphold its legacy. My welcome followed the standard protocol for high-altitude areas – simple dining in, just a warm handshake, and a smooth handover from the previous CO.

The next day, I met the Corps Chief Engineer, a hulking figure whose gravelly voice always sounded as if he was battling a stubborn cough, perhaps a souvenir from his long stint in the area. "Welcome to the station! Your regiment is doing an excellent job. Carry on with the same josh!" he declared.

Later, the Chief of Staff (COS) called me to his office. A no-nonsense man, he laid out the grand plan. "We want Khardung La to be re-laid. New shelters, retaining works, a temple, a memorial, a café, a souvenir room, and a grand flag post displaying the Tricolor and our formation flags. Simultaneously, the baggage handling area at the airport requires a complete overhaul – waiting areas, X-ray machines, scanners, the works! And all this must be accomplished before your regiment moves out."

I gulped. This wasn't just a task; it was an engineering marathon at an altitude where even breathing felt like an achievement.

But Sappers never back down. My team got cracking, working day and night. Every alternate day, I drove up to Khardung La, an arduous 2.5-hour journey one way – supervising every detail. The regiment was determined to prove its mettle, and the progress was swift.

By the end of August, the transformation was complete. What was once a chaotic, haphazard place now looked like a pristine, tourist-friendly zone. To mark the occasion, my wife, both daughters, and a few officers with their wives joined me for a picnic at Khardung La.

As we sipped coffee, standing in the sun outside the newly opened café, a young foreign couple approached us. The guy, sensing some measure of authority in our presence, remarked, "We were here years ago, and it looked nothing like this! We heard the Army revamped it in no time."

He then did something that caught me off guard – he asked for my autograph!

Suppressing a grin, I took his notepad and inscribed, "Army Engineers who re-laid Khardung La are incredible. Cherry on the top – the Bengal Sappers and my regiment made it happen in record time!" The couple read it with fascination, nodding in admiration.

Meanwhile, the baggage handling area neared completion, pending only the arrival of high-tech security equipment. Just as we were wrapping up, the COS announced the dreaded Annual Adm Inspection. Every regiment feared his scrutiny; his sharp eyes spared no fault. As he made his rounds through our unit, he maintained perfect silence. No rebukes, no nitpicking. He simply inspected every corner, then was ready to leave without having uttered a single word.

I braced myself for the worst. But as he departed, he turned to me and said, "I hope the regiment relieving you is just as good."

Coming from a man nicknamed 'Non-Smiling', this was equivalent to receiving a medallion! My chest swelled with pride.

As our tenure wrapped up, Corps HQ initiated a citation for the regiment's outstanding work. It sailed through without a hitch, a rare occurrence in Army bureaucracy! The citation wasn't solely for those two projects but for the regiment's exceptional performance during its entire tenure in the high-altitude region. Every officer, JCO, and soldier truly deserved recognition for their steadfast dedication.

Years later, in an almost cinematic twist of fate, I was posted as Centre Commandant, just as the Colonel Commandant had predicted. His words, spoken in passing, had become reality.

In retrospect, I realized that destiny's winding road often leads to places we never envisioned. But when walked with conviction, it unveils grander designs than we dare to imagine.

तेरी मेहनत ने रंग और नूर दिया मुझको,
वो अनकहे अल्फ़ाज़ मेरा इश्क़ बन गए हैं।
मगर तक़दीर का फलसफा तो देखो,
तकरार से बचने की जो बातें कभी की उसने,
आज वही हक़ीक़त मेरी हसीन यादें बन गई हैं।

THE BRAINSTORMING MARCH TO MATHURA

Some formation commanders have a knack for keeping their units busy. It's as if they fear free time might lead to an existential crisis, or worse, a coup! Their method? Assign, micromanage, repeat.

Before I took command of my regiment at Leh in early 2005, our next station was already known. It was Mathura, the birthplace of Lord Krishna. Within months, the advance parties of both the relieving unit and mine moved, kicking off the high-stakes ritual of handing over and taking over. Chaos in the making!

But here's the thing about moving a regiment. After the initial madness of handing over, there's a stretch of about two months that is relatively lean. Not a vacation - convoy movements, logistics, and settling in the new station are no easy tasks - but compared to our usual high-altitude grind, this felt like a breather.

Or so I thought.

One fine June morning, I checked in with the Commander, Engineer Brigade, under whose formation we were to serve in Mathura. Ever the good soldier, I started with pleasantries. "Sir, we are delighted to be coming under your command. The regiment has done outstanding work here, and we will leave no stone unturned at the new station."

Before this, I had already sent a DO letter outlining our commendable work in the high-altitude area and our planned move. I expected a nod of approval. However, his response threw me off. "Yes, I am aware of your regiment's performance. But tell me, how do you plan to keep your officers busy during the two-month move and initial settling-in period?"

Busy? Wasn't the move itself a logistical nightmare?

I fumbled. "Sir, coordinating the move, managing convoys, and setting up at Mathura will keep us quite occupied."

He remained unimpressed. "That's routine. Officers have fertile minds. When they have time, they start thinking... differently. I suggest you use this period intellectually. Take up a study, work on it during the move, and present it once you settle in Mathura."

Then came the masterstroke. *"The topic will be: India's Military Responses to Pakistan's Asymmetric War Being Waged at All Planes."*

I nearly choked. A weighty topic, utterly unrelated to our engineering tasks. But orders were orders. I called my scholarly Company Commander and a youngster to get cracking while I assumed an overall guide role.

"Sir," the Company Commander said with a smirk, "I bet the Corps Commander gave this to the Brigade Commander, and he's just passing it down to us."

I nodded grimly. "Possibly. But we still have to do it."

While most units spent their move enjoying movies and exploring markets, we drowned ourselves in research. Internet access was spotty, so we relied on libraries, expert consultations, and whatever strategic wisdom we could squeeze from the Corps HQ.

One officer at the Corps HQ raised an eyebrow when I requested reference materials. "Why are you so obsessed with asymmetric warfare? Shouldn't you be focusing on your move?"

I had no answer.

By September, as we moved from Leh to Pathankot by road convoy, our journey had turned into an academic grind. At Pathankot, where we stayed for a few days tying up arrangements for the military special train, meal timings became debate sessions. By the time we boarded the train to Mathura, our journey had transformed into a rolling seminar. Our version of entertainment? Heated discussions on military doctrines while other units enjoyed Bollywood flicks.

Just as we neared the finish line, fate intervened.

The Engineer Brigade Commander, the mastermind of this brilliant assignment, was posted abroad before we even reached Mathura! By the time we settled in, a new Brigade Commander had taken over.

Could we drop the study? What a ridiculous notion. The Brigade HQ staff, in their typical backhanded style, took immense pleasure in tracking our every step, ensuring we remained buried under work.

Then came the final twist. An official letter announced that in the upcoming Formation Commanders' Conference, a 20-minute slot had been reserved for our regiment's presentation. The GOC himself would be in attendance.

I had no choice but to step up. Our study was polished, neatly spiral-bound, and ready. On the big day, I delivered the presentation with PowerPoint slides, supporting data, and carefully selected visuals. When I finished, silence filled the hall. Then, a sudden burst of appreciation. Several formation commanders remarked, "A fabulous study and presentation!"

As the GOC exited, he patted me on the shoulder. That moment made all our sleepless nights and book-filled journeys worthwhile. Word spread around. Everyone knew that this new regiment had not only settled in swiftly but had also left an intellectual mark within weeks of arrival. Our already strong reputation from Leh was now etched in stone.

Later, I discovered that this study wasn't a task handed down from the Corps Commander to the Brigade Commander, as we had assumed. It was entirely the Brigade Commander's own brainchild - a visionary move to set the tone for our arrival.

At first, it felt like an unnecessary burden. But in hindsight, I realized that sometimes, bizarre orders have hidden benefits. What seemed like extra hassle during our move became our golden ticket to intellectual stardom in the new formation. And if nothing else, I can proudly say that I once spent the entire move period buried in books instead of Bollywood movies. Now, that's what I call action-packed!

राह-ए-इश्क़ आसान नहीं,
हर लम्हा इक आज़माइश थी।
सज़ा दर सज़ा दी तुमने यूं,
कि अफ़साना-ए-मुहब्बत ख़ूबसूरत बनी।

FIRST-CLASS LESSON IN ENTITLEMENTS

"मेरा कुत्ता कुत्ता, तेरा कुत्ता टॉमी?" (My dog is just ordinary, but your dog is special.) This popular dialogue from a TV serial flashed through my mind as I sat down to write this story.

During my tenure as the CO of an engineer regiment in Mathura, I frequently travelled to Bathinda to attend conferences at the Engineer Brigade HQ. These quarterly meetings were essential for discussing important training matters, unit adm, and dissemination of vital directions from higher HQ. They also provided a platform for unit commanders to exchange ideas, streamline coordination, and learn from each other's best practices.

While I sometimes took a cab, my preferred mode of travel was the Punjab Mail. I would board at around 7 in the evening, catch a 6-7 hour sleep, and arrive at Bathinda at 3 in the morning, refreshed and ready for usually a half-day-long session of deliberations, followed by a working lunch. By late evening, I would board the return train and be back with my regiment the next morning.

As per custom, my Subedar Major (SM) would see me off at the railway station, and my orderly, who travelled in a different compartment, accompanied me for any adm support. This was standard practice, ensuring smooth travel and readiness for the meetings ahead.

One such evening, as I settled into my first-class AC coupe, my SM ensured my bags were properly placed before bidding me a crisp salute. I then noticed my fellow passenger, a gentleman of my age, already making himself comfortable.

"I work with Indian Railways, a 'Group A' officer," he introduced himself. "I have a house in Mathura but work in Delhi. Heading to Bathinda on official duty."

We exchanged pleasantries, and as the train gained speed, our conversation became more engaging. He spoke at length about the critical role railways played in the nation's transportation network, their challenges, and the responsibilities that came with it. I, too, had my share of experiences to narrate, and soon, small talk turned into an animated discussion about public services and governance.

As dinner time approached, my orderly arrived with my continental meal, neatly packed in Tiffin from the Officers' Mess. My co-passenger had a simpler meal, but with an added indulgence, a bottle of whisky.

"How about a drink?" he offered, pouring himself a generous peg.

"Thanks, but I don't drink," I replied with a polite smile.

As we dined, the conversation took an interesting turn. With a smirk, he remarked, "You defence guys have it easy, orderlies at your beck and call, VIP treatment everywhere, and of course, the best perk, subsidized liquor from the canteen. And that too, foreign brands! Must be nice."

I could sense the sarcasm. I usually have patience until provoked. Smilingly, I clarified, "Nothing comes free. We pay for what we get, and the subsidy is recognition of the hardships and sacrifices of service life."

But he wasn't done yet. "Still, I think the government is a bit too generous with your perks," he added, swirling his drink.

There was no point in dragging the debate further, so I simply wished him goodnight and went to sleep.

Early in the morning, as I stepped out of the train, my railway companion, now in a much friendlier tone, made an unexpected request.

"You know, I often visit Mathura. If you could get me a few bottles of Scotch from your canteen, I'd be happy to pick them up from your place - of course, paying for them."

I smiled inwardly. Here was a man who had just criticized military privileges, now eager to enjoy them. I decided to return the favour.

"I remember you mentioning your recent family trip to Trivandrum using free railway passes. I'm planning a trip down South. Could you arrange some passes for me?"

His face turned pale. "Uh... those are for railway personnel only."

"Exactly! Just as subsidized canteen items are meant for defence personnel," I replied, patting his shoulder.

The expression on his face was priceless, somewhere between realization and embarrassment.

As I walked away, I chuckled to myself. It was amusing how people often failed to see their own entitlements as privileges while being quick to question those of others. These benefits, whether in the railways or the military, were not personal luxuries but institutional provisions meant to aid professional efficiency. It was our responsibility to ensure they were not misused.

And as I reflected on the irony of it all, the very first dialogue at the beginning echoed in my head once more: **"मेरा कुत्ता कुत्ता, तेरा कुत्ता टॉमी?"** It perfectly captured his attitude - his entitlements were justified, but mine were excessive. How strange!!

CAMOUFLAGE AND CONCEALMENT SERVED ON THE ROCKS

"Fire in the belly and passion in the heart" - that's the very fuel that keeps an Army soldier marching, whether through icy terrains or into a gathering of polished shoes and gleaming glasses. The motto I first heard at the Army War College as a Directing Staff (DS) has stayed with me ever since. This spirit isn't reserved just for operations; it flows seamlessly into our celebrations too. After all, if there's one thing the Army never misses besides hitting targets - it's an opportunity to raise a toast, share laughter, and create memories that outlast the hangovers.

After assuming command of the elitist outfit of the Bengal Sappers, I found myself at the helm in Leh in March 2005 - my fourth engineer unit after commissioning, and indeed a rare fortune for an engineer officer to serve in so many units. Having braved the high altitudes, I was soon entrusted with the task of de-inducting my regiment to a peace station.

Mathura welcomed us with open arms and, as expected, presented a fresh set of challenges because, let's be honest, peace stations are never truly peaceful in the Army. The Corps HQ was conveniently (or inconveniently) next door, which meant additional duties. But as they say, "Why fear extra duties when you've already survived Leh's chill?"

It was the wedding anniversary of our Corps Commander. Naturally, a grand cocktail party was organized at the Flag Staff House - a place every YO dreams of occupying someday. The invite was extended to all station unit commanders, their better halves, and of course, the privileged club of senior officers fondly known as the 'Navratnas'.

Now, when an invite from a senior officer says cocktail evening, it means exactly 60 minutes - no more, no less. That's military precision for you.

Dressed in formal attire, my wife and I arrived right on time - me carrying a well-wrapped bottle of wine, and my wife, a bouquet of roses, an elegant offering for the gracious hostess. Soon, the Navratnas arrived, looking like walking advertisements for luxury fashion, all carrying their own tokens of goodwill. The GOC and his wife, along with his ever-alert ADC, greeted each guest personally on their sprawling lawn. The air soon filled with hearty greetings and laughter.

Like any big Army gathering, the catering staff was pooled from various unit messes. From my regiment too, a smart, wide-eyed waiter had been deputed, assigned the task of attending to me and a handful of other officers and their spouses. He knew my taste - especially the fact that I was a non-drinker. Over time, he'd perfected the art of serving me my signature drink without me uttering a word.

As the gathering settled, drinks and snacks began to flow like clockwork. My regiment's loyal waiter soon appeared with my usual drink - Appy Fizz, artfully diluted with ice cubes, served in a crystal tumbler that could easily pass for a whisky glass. The camouflage was flawless. Around me, single malts and cocktails sparkled under the lights, but I sipped my disguised fizz with utmost composure.

The Corps Chief Engineer soon drifted towards our group, sipping his single malt - a drink he indulged in only occasionally. Noticing my glass, he arched an eyebrow but said nothing - perhaps silently appreciating my 'choice' of drink. Conversations flowed from mundane matters to the latest buzz dominating casual chatter - recently introduced

YouTube and Facebook, making them the highlights of light-hearted exchanges that evening.

Ten minutes in, my glass was empty. The ADC, ever watchful, swooped in. "Sir, this won't do. How often do you get to have a drink in the GOC's house?" he chided playfully before signalling my waiter for a refill. Dutifully, the waiter arrived with another round of my special - again, Appy Fizz diluted with ice, masquerading as premium whisky.

As the evening progressed, the GOC himself made rounds, insisting everyone top up their drinks. I gulped down my second drink swiftly to make room for the third. "Sir, I'll surely have another drink - I dare not say no to the GOC," I declared with theatrical enthusiasm. My waiter, a master of silent service, returned promptly with yet another fizzy concoction, this time without diluting it. However, the GOC squinted at the glass and joked, "Mind diluting its concentration?"

Without missing a beat, I asked the waiter to add soda and more ice. Imagine that - Appy Fizz with soda. A mix even the most adventurous bartender wouldn't dare create! But there I was, sipping it like it had been aged in oak barrels.

After an hour of such spirited drinking, we bid farewell to our gracious hosts. The Chief Engineer's knowing glances lingered, but I carried my secret home, snug in the folds of Army decorum and personal deception.

Fast forward to April 2007 - our regiment's Raising Day celebrations were in full swing. The grand finale was the Officers' Mess social, attended by the same senior officers, including the Corps Commander, the Navratnas, and yes, the sharp-eyed Chief Engineer. As the evening unfolded, I stood confidently with a glass of dark Pepsi, blending seamlessly into the crowd of whisky enthusiasts.

But the Chief Engineer wasn't letting me off so easily. Spotting me, he roared, "CO Saab, you're making others drunk while holding a soft drink. Come on, ask for your Scotch!" I laughed politely. "Sir, I don't take hard drinks."

His eyes twinkled with mischief. "Since when have you started lying? At the GOC's party, you downed glass after glass of your favourite whisky. The speed and concentration with which you enjoyed it amazed me. I know you've got tremendous capacity!"

I smiled, realizing that revealing my deception would only ruin the masterpiece of camouflage I'd crafted. After all, 'camouflage and concealment' was the forte of the Corps of Engineers, and I was practically duty-bound to possess it!

It was then I realized that, fortunately or unfortunately, my craft in camouflage and concealment, honed so meticulously, was bound to catch up with me someday and cause a big embarrassment. So, occasionally, I started to indulge in a thoughtful sip of brandy - purely for health reasons, of course, as advised by the doctors!!

हकीकत से दूर ही रहूँ तो अच्छा है,
अक्सर सच्चाई में झूठ छिपा होता है।

HUSBANDS' NIGHT AND THE 'OPTIONAL' DRESS CODE

Army parties have a unique charm - extravagant, meticulously planned, and executed with military precision. The effort that goes into organizing these events is unparalleled. From the menu to the décor, every detail is thoughtfully curated, making the celebrations grand and unforgettable. Officers and their wives work in perfect harmony, ensuring that the event is nothing short of spectacular.

Back in 2006, I was commanding an Engineer Regiment in Mathura, which was part of an Engineer Brigade headquartered in Bathinda, along with two other regiments. The Brigade's specialist regiment was based in Ambala. That April, we were gearing up for a massive Corps-level EWT - a high-stakes formation exercise designed to test the operational readiness of the entire Corps. The preparation was intense, demanding rigorous training, flawless coordination, and unwavering commitment.

For nearly two months, under the scorching heat in the deserts, we practiced relentlessly. Officers and men alike shed sweat - and at least a couple of kilos - perfecting our combat engineering skills and battle procedures. Back at our unit locations, the wives held the fort, managing affairs and planning something special for our return.

As we were wrapping up the exercise and preparing to move back to our garrisons, a beautifully crafted invitation arrived. The ladies of the Brigade had jointly planned a welcome-back party for their husbands, themed 'Husbands' Night'. The invitation was elegantly worded, adorned with heartfelt poetry, and carried a touch of emotion. It mentioned the time, venue, and most interestingly, the dress code:

"For Gentlemen - Traditional as per theme." "For Ladies - Optional."

The wording seemed fine, and no one paid much attention to it at that time.

A few days later, after returning from the exercise, we all geared up for the much-anticipated event. Officers from different regiments arrived in Bathinda, dressed in their finest traditional attire - kurta-pajamas, dhotis, lungis, Kerala mundus, Maratha outfits, and even North-Eastern ensembles.

At the venue entrance, the ladies stood in a line, welcoming us with aarti and flower petals. It was a touching and emotional gesture. Inside, the atmosphere was electric. The wives had put up spectacular performances - music, dance, and even skits. Party games involving the husbands added to the fun. The food, lovingly prepared by the ladies themselves, was exceptional. Drinks flowed freely, and laughter filled the air.

As if it's customary in such gatherings, after an hour or so, natural groups started forming - senior officers with their wives in one corner, junior officers in another, and bachelors having their own lively discussions. In one such senior officers' group sat the Brigade Commander, his wife, and the COs of the regiments with their spouses.

The party was in full swing when one of the COs, known for his sharp wit and keen observation, suddenly went quiet. He was intently staring at the invitation, which was pinned to a board nearby. After a few moments, he smirked and said, "Does anyone find anything odd about this invitation?"

Everyone turned to look at the card, but nothing seemed amiss.

"Come on, it's beautifully written, with great poetry too," someone remarked.

"Yes, of course," the CO replied, "but focus on the dress code."

We all leaned in to read again.

"For Gentlemen - Traditional as per theme." "For Ladies Optional."

A brief silence. Then, as the realization hit, a thunderous burst of laughter echoed across the lawn.

"OPTIONAL??"

The implications of that innocent wording sent the entire group into hysterics. The ladies sitting with the senior officers shook their heads with amused smiles, some raising their eyebrows as if to say, 'Men will be men'! The Brigade Commander, suppressing his chuckles, remarked, "Well, I guess it's time for dinner now!"

The Husbands' Night concluded as a resounding success, with laughter, great food, and unforgettable moments. But that one word "Optional" remained etched in our memories, a private joke that never failed to bring a smile.

खुदा भी हँस पड़ेगा हमारी मासूमियत पे,
जो सोचते हैं कि महफ़िलों में ग़लतफ़हमियाँ नहीं होती!

THE ARMY'S GREAT LEVELLER

The Army life is like a grand illusion. One day, you're sipping single malt in a crystal tumbler, the next; you're gulping down a tot of rum in an enamel mug. One day, a fleet of vehicles with saluting drivers is at your beck and call, the next; you're desperately searching for transport that even remotely resembles an official vehicle. The unpredictability is relentless, but every officer learns to embrace it with a smile.

After years of hard work and dedication, I had the privilege of commanding an elite Engineer Regiment, a dream every young officer cherishes. The thrill of absolute authority, a dedicated staff ensuring even my coffee was brewed to perfection, and the satisfaction of seeing my unit excel in every endeavour was unmatched. The icing on the cake? A unit citation during my tenure.

Then came my next posting as a DS at the Army War College, Mhow. As the news spread, congratulatory messages poured in. "Sir, this is a stepping stone!" "Well deserved, Sir!" "A prestigious appointment, Sir!" The officers demanded a party, and I obliged, basking in the warmth of my grand farewell.

My orderly was despatched ahead with my luggage and our family dog, expecting the usual regimental reception - a platoon ready to offload the Commanding Officer's baggage. But the War College had different ideas. No welcoming party, no platoon, just a blank stare from the Camp Office.

"You'll have to arrange civil labour for unloading," came the indifferent response from the Camp Commandant. My poor orderly, used to clockwork precision, was in for a rude awakening. Scrambling with his signature 'personal charisma,' he managed to get a few labourers, only for an unexpected downpour to drench my luggage and my bewildered dog.

The next day, I landed in Indore with my wife and daughters, expecting a crisp, saluting driver in a gleaming Gypsy. Instead, my orderly, now thoroughly disillusioned, was informed that officers on posting had to wait for the station bus. "Station bus?!" he sputtered.

Accustomed to grand farewells with trumpets, this was an existential crisis for him. With no choice, I waited an hour before being picked up by an old station bus with a speed governor seemingly locked at 40.

At my temporary accommodation, my orderly stood teary-eyed. "Sir, ye aap kahan aa gaye?" (Sir, where have you come?), he murmured in despair. I patted his shoulder, grinning, "Welcome to the War College, buddy. Every DS here has been a CO, and has enjoyed all privileges. This is how things work."

The next day, my official transport arrived, a vintage Armada Jeep driven by a civilian in khaki, unshaven, with a paunch that threatened the steering wheel. He was tasked with taking me to the Station HQ and various locations in the town for my immediate adm requirements. My orderly nearly sent him back with a reprimand, but before he could, I calmly boarded. "Let's go," I said.

For three days, my once-vibrant orderly was silent, shell-shocked by the 'new normal'. Soon, word reached my Regiment. The SM called, concerned, "Sir, we thought this was a prestigious posting, but your orderly says it's a punishment! What's going on, Sir?" I reassured him, laughing, "SM Saab, this is just the Army's way of showing us all shades of life. Tell the boys all is well."

The Adjutant called next, voice brimming with emotion. "Sir, I know you'll say NO, but we're not asking. We are sending your cook immediately. We can't imagine Ma'am managing without him and any adm staff!"

Despite my protests, a cook was despatched. Within a month, life at the War College found its rhythm. I drove my own new Maruti SX4 to the office, but for outdoor exercises, I hopped into the infamous Armada with my DS colleagues. My orderly, now adjusted, found solace in the deep respect the DS body commanded from student officers.

One day, he sheepishly admitted, "Sir, mujhe pehle laga ki aapko ye punishment posting mili hai, lekin ab lagta hai yeh jagah kuch alag hi hai. Jo izzat DS ko milti hai voh kahin naseeb nahin ho sakti." (Sir, I first thought this was your punishment posting, but now I realize this place is something else! The respect a DS gets here is unmatched!)

That's the beauty of Army life. It teaches you to embrace every turn with a smile. One day, you're a VIP on the golf course, the next; you're ensuring its bunkers are well maintained. One day, you're enjoying the luxury of a bungalow, the next; you're sleeping under the stars.

This ability to adapt to any situation, good, bad, or ugly, is what truly defines an Army guy. It is more than a skill; it is a way of life shaped by years of service. While everyone learns resilience differently, Army life instills unmatched flexibility, a sense of purpose in every role, and dignity in all circumstances. This is what its true beauty is!

तुम क्या जानो तन्हाई का लुत्फ़ क्या होता है,
जो शाम-ए-महफ़िल हमेशा गुलज़ार में कटी हो।

WHEN MODERN WARFARE COLLIDED WITH MEDIEVAL TACTICS

Every new tenure in the Army is like stepping into a different world, bringing fresh experiences and countless lessons. The Army War College, Mhow, was no different. My nearly three-year stint from 2007 to 2010 was an unforgettable chapter, filled with interactions that made even the most seasoned and elderly officers feel a few years younger.

The DS body was all battle-hardened officers, each having commanded their units with pride and flair. With backgrounds covering infantry, artillery, mechanized forces, technical arms, and logistics, they brought diverse perspectives to the table. Some were serious, others light-hearted, and a few had their own quirky methods of imparting wisdom.

One particularly unique DS from Maratha Light Infantry stood out. He had an impressive operational record, having survived multiple bullet injuries in combat. His experience was unparalleled, his passion for teaching unmatched - but his methodology was unconventional.

For him, military tactics weren't just drills and procedures; they were ancient art forms. His classes on modern warfare often took unexpected detours into Shivaji's guerrilla tactics, Chanakya-Niti, and even medieval siege strategies. If you walked past his classroom, you'd think a battlefield commander was rallying his troops rather than conducting a lesson. His voice could be heard from multiple classrooms away, often drowning out the other discussions in progress.

One day, during a division-level Sand Model Discussion (SMD) on "road opening in counter insurgency environment", nearly

80 officers sat, eager to absorb insights. True to his style, our beloved DS took the floor - and history came alive.

"Gentlemen, before we discuss modern road-opening tactics, let me take you back to the era when Shivaji employed his legendary strategies in the Western Ghats..."

For nearly an hour, students were treated to a masterclass in historical warfare, with little relevance to the actual topic. The SI, a seasoned veteran himself, silently entered the room, observed the unfolding spectacle, and left - his displeasure visible to all.

The next morning, during the weekly DS prayer, a formal session where key teaching points were discussed - the atmosphere was unusually tense. The SI arrived early, an ominous sign.

After everyone had presented their topics for the upcoming week, he walked up to the rostrum, paused, and scanned the room. Then, in a calm yet authoritative tone, he delivered his verdict:

"Gentlemen, you are all experienced officers, having commanded your units with distinction. But there is a time and place for philosophical discussions. This course is about 'what' needs to be done - drills and procedures. The 'why' and 'why not' comes later, in senior courses. We are here to create tactically sound young officers, not future Army Chiefs debating medieval warfare! Please ensure that discussions remain focused and strictly as per the lesson plans."

His words were direct, the message crystal clear. Our history-obsessed DS sat, fuming but silent.

What followed became legend. Our loud-mouthed DS, unwavering in his ways, was said to have marched straight to the SI, expressing his discontent. He defended his methods, citing his unmatched experience and battle-hardened wisdom.

As the saying goes, some habits are too deep-rooted to die. Despite the SI's advice, the officer remained steadfast, drawing from the rich tapestry of his experiences and his undying love for ancient strategy. The SI, perhaps recognizing the futility of change, allowed the officer to continue his idiosyncratic approach. His legacy, though unconventional, lived on, fondly remembered by all. Ah, the good old days!"

कुछ बात है कि हस्ती मिटती नहीं हमारी,
सदियों रहा है दुश्मन दौर-ए-जहाँ हमारा।

<u>SMARTNESS GONE WRONG</u>

At the Army War College, senior officers visited every now and then, and their arrivals were marked by grand ceremonial parties - lavish lunches or formal dinners. A handful of DS from each Wing were nominated to attend, adding just the right mix of decorum, and occasionally unintended entertainment. These weren't your everyday officers. The DS body was a distinguished league of veterans, each with decades of experience under their belts. They had commanded units with distinction, navigated the trickiest terrains, served on international assignments, and some even wore gallantry awards as literal badges of honour. Casual remarks, especially those questioning their competence, were strictly off-limits.

During the annual adm inspection of the College in 2008, a very high ranking flag officer arrived from Lucknow on behalf of his boss to scrutinize every aspect of adm, observing instructional processes with a hawk's eye. His reputation preceded him - not exactly admirable, but certainly known.

On the second day of the inspection, his boss, himself arrived. His visit was more ceremonial, topped off with a formal dinner. The day unfolded with tours of various Wings, a leisurely drive around the campus, and the evening highlight - a round of golf, followed by the grand dinner at the Officers' Mess. The ante-room, as expansive as a tennis court, set the perfect stage for mingling and small talk.

The dinner, attended by the War College Commandant, senior staff officers, and a select DS body from all Wings (including me), was expected to maintain an air of dignity. It was a stag event.

As the evening progressed with the drinks flowing, the flag officer who conducted the inspection on the first day, decided to sprinkle some 'wisdom' while chatting with a group of DS. Trying to impress his boss, he casually remarked, "While the instructional abilities of the DS body are commendable, their physical fitness clearly leaves much to be desired." It was meant to be clever, but it wasn't.

The boss, known for his hyperactive personality and impressive fitness, couldn't resist biting back. Turning to one of the DS, a war hero no less, he sarcastically said, "I am 100% with what he just said. Have you ever looked at yourself in the mirror? You look like a HALWAI."

Now, how could a gallantry award winner, a man who had faced insurgents head-on, tolerate such a disrespectful and absurd comment? In an instant, the DS pulled his shirt out of his trousers, lifted it up to his tummy, and just before anyone could stop him from lifting it further, revealed scars etched across his torso - battle wounds from an operation in the Northeast.

"Sir, take a good look. I got this fighting insurgents. I survived after spending two months in the military hospital," he retorted, his voice laced with anger.

But he wasn't done. Still seething, he added, "Despite being in a low medical category, I outperformed most officers during PT yesterday. Maybe someone missed that part of the inspection."

The room grew tense, thick with discomfort. But the boss, his ego bruised, wasn't one to back down. "I've fought insurgents too," he responded. "But I still look fit, unlike you. Let's settle this, right here, right now. We'll crawl across the length of this ante-room. Whoever loses eats CROW MEAT."

Before the ante-room could turn into an impromptu wrestling arena, the Commandant intervened, steering the boss to a quieter corner with the finesse of someone used to diffusing such awkwardness. The flag officer who had sparked the fire had conveniently vanished, no doubt realizing his attempt to score points had spectacularly backfired.

In hindsight, the whole fiasco was avoidable. The officer's comment was reckless, and the boss's reaction, though impulsive, only fanned the flames. It was a textbook case of how some senior officers, in their misguided attempts to act 'smart,' end up exposing their own glaring flaws. In the process, they bruise egos, trample on self-respect, and more often than not, end up with their foot in their mouth.

As I reflect on that evening, I'm reminded of a wise CO who once, while pipping ranks on a young officer, said, "It's easy to grow here," pointing to the shoulders, "but much harder to grow here," tapping his temple. "So, always strive to develop the upper faculty."

यूँ ना शोहरत-ए-जशन तू मना ख़ातिब,
सबने देखा है हुसूल-ए-मक़सद पाने का,
तेरा तरीक़ा मुकम्मल।

SUPREMO'S SURPRISE : WHEN AVAILABILITY TRUMPED ABILITY

At the Army War College, each Wing had its own senior-most DS, an officer who, by virtue of tenure rather than seniority, enjoyed a special status. In the JC Wing, he was called 'Supremo'. Unlike the younger DS who toiled away guiding student officers, Supremo had a different role. He was not burdened with routine academic duties but was instead a source of wisdom, humour, and the occasional well-timed piece of advice.

Towards the end of 2009, our Supremo was a legend. A proud infantry officer with a razor-sharp wit, he could make even the most serious commanders crack a smile. He was well-liked, well-respected, and most importantly, well aware of how to enjoy his privileged position.

Then came a new Commander, a man of formidable intellect and relentless energy. He had a deep passion for academic rigor and believed that the DS body should not only be intellectually equipped but also develop a clear, analytical approach to complex issues. To this end, he frequently assigned book reviews, research topics, and studies. No one was exempt. Supremo had, so far, remained untouched by these scholarly demands.

Until one fine day.

A central forum was approaching, where DS from all Wings would present and debate current military issues before the Commandant. The topic assigned to the Wing was complex, requiring deep research and domain expertise. Supremo, known more for his quick wit than for PowerPoint slides, seemed an unlikely choice for the task. But the Commander had other plans.

Calling Supremo to his office, he said, "Supremo, I know this isn't your area of expertise. Traditionally, you're not given these assignments. But this is a key event, and every DS is already committed."

Supremo, ever the cheerful sport, grinned. "Of course, Sir! Consider it done."

The fact that he had no background in the subject did not seem to concern him. While others dived into books and research papers, Supremo carried on as usual, appearing relaxed and unbothered. Some wondered if he had resigned himself to fate, while others suspected he had a trick up his sleeve. The day of reckoning was shortly to arrive.

The Wing gathered for a rehearsal, with the Commander watching closely. Supremo walked up to the podium, connected his presentation, and took a deep breath.

Then, with a twinkle in his eye, he began. "Gentlemen, let me be honest. Don't expect groundbreaking insights from me today. I wasn't given this topic because of my ABILITY but because of my AVAILABILITY."

The room burst into laughter. Even the Commander, known for his serious approach, couldn't help but smile. But then, something unexpected happened. Supremo, who had just downplayed his role with a joke, went on to deliver a presentation so sharp, so well-structured, and so engaging that it left everyone speechless. What started as an amusing anecdote turned into a lesson in preparation, intelligence, and the power of humour.

The takeaway? Many times, a person's easygoing attitude, or even self-effacing remarks may lead others to believe that they are not serious contenders in high-stakes intellectual or professional arenas. But appearances can be misleading. True capability often resides behind an unassuming facade. When someone truly competent claims to be unqualified, chances are they are the best person for the job!

And as fate would have it, I too became the Supremo in 2010, about six months before completing my tenure. But before that, I had already presented a study at the central forum - one that I had worked on while commanding an Engineer Regiment. It had earned accolades then, and guess what? It earned even bigger applause here in the War College!

अंदाज़ा फ़रेब खा गया मेरे सलीके का,
लोगों ने देखकर मुझे मामूली समझ लिया।

THE GLOBE-TROTTING MIRAGE

After an invigorating tenure at Mhow, where I had the privilege of engaging with sharp, inquisitive minds brimming with questions and ideas, I wasn't left brooding for long. I was handpicked in 2010 for my next assignment as the Director in the prestigious Combat Engineers Directorate under the E-in-C's branch. My new role was anything but routine. I was entrusted with the critical responsibility of 'prospective planning of engineer equipment' for the Corps of Engineers.

The responsibility was immense. I had to dive deep into qualitative requirements, stay abreast of the operational relevance of in-service equipment, evaluate the future needs of field formations, and anticipate how emerging technologies could reshape combat engineering - all to ensure well-considered, strategic procurement decisions. Regular interactions with Defence Research & Development Organisation (DRDO) were part of the job to gauge indigenous capabilities, along with constant reviews of global trends through defence expos, military journals, and interactions with foreign manufacturers. To do justice to this role, I had two capable officers working directly under me.

One of our immediate critical projects involved evaluating two equipment that were essential for modern, high-mobility engineer operations and under consideration for import. After thorough internal assessments, the ministry had approved the necessity for these systems, clearing the path for us to conduct foreign visits to USA and a few other countries to witness live demonstrations. The team was to include the Engineer-in-Chief (E-in-C), an officer from the Weapons & Equipment (WE) Directorate, and me. Our white passports arrived, visas stamped, and tickets booked. It seemed like we were all set.

But that's when the real battle began - not on foreign soil, but within the labyrinth of bureaucratic corridors.

The seemingly straightforward file, containing all necessary approvals, started its slow pilgrimage through various desks. It eventually landed on the desk of the Joint Secretary (JS), where it stayed put like an immovable rock, growing thicker with each round of observations and clarifications - eventually outweighing the very equipment we intended to procure.

With just a few days left before our scheduled departure, I received a call from the JS: "If the E-in-C wants this visit cleared, he should come and meet the Defence Secretary to clarify the doubts."

I conveyed this to the E-in-C, expecting him to agree to a meeting. But his response was firm and laced with understated wisdom: "Kats, we've spent months addressing every query. The necessity has already been approved on file, and you've personally clarified all doubts. If they still need 'ego massage', perhaps they never intended to approve it. Give it one last try yourself, but don't chase shadows."

Nevertheless, I made one last attempt the next morning. The JS greeted me with the now infamous file, flipping through it. Pointing to a fresh observation from the Defence Secretary, he read aloud with an expression that blended seriousness with subtle amusement: "From the officers' biodata, it's evident they've already visited several foreign countries. Why do they need to travel again? Can't the manufacturers bring their equipment here? This seems more like a globe-trotting exercise than an operational necessity."

I couldn't help bursting into laughter at the globe-trotting remark. The JS looked up, half-amused, half-surprised. I explained, between chuckles, that our previous foreign visits were purely academic during training courses - entirely different from operational evaluations. As for manufacturers bringing equipment here? Not feasible. They'd already declined, citing logistical challenges and, frankly, their aversion to navigating the notorious Indian bureaucratic maze.

The JS nodded sympathetically. "I understand, but you know how the system works," he said, shrugging with the resigned grace of a man who's seen many files come and go, but rarely the people they represent.

When I returned to brief the E-in-C, he listened quietly. Then, with a wry smile, he said: "So, Kats, we're officially globe-trotters now! It seems we've mastered everything except the art of convincing minds that enjoy the maze more than the destination."

We both laughed, but beneath the humour was a shared frustration. It wasn't about the missed trip; it was the realization that our modernization efforts were often marred not by a lack of professional competence, but because of bureaucratic red tape wrapped tightly around decision-making.

Years later, even after his retirement, whenever we met, the E-in-C would nudge me and say with a grin: "Kats, because of me, you missed your globe-trotting mission!"

लियाकत तो थी बेशुमार उसमें, बस इल्म न था जीहज़ूरी का,
आख़िर यही वजह बनी, उल्फ़त-ए-रुसवाई की।

LOST IN EUROPE, FOUND IN INDIA

There's something magical about the words 'foreign visit'. They evoke images of exotic lands, dazzling skylines, and if you're in the Army, an absurd amount of paperwork.

After our previous failed 'globe-trotting' mission, fate decided to be kind. I was soon slated to visit not just one, but three European countries - Czech Republic, Poland, and Austria. As a part of my role in the Combat Engineers' Directorate, I was tasked with inspecting equipment essential for our field formations. You see, as the saying goes: "Plan not for an adversary's intentions, but for their capabilities." The motto was clear: stay ahead, stay sharp. And apparently, stay jet-lagged!

Interestingly, approvals for our visit went seamlessly and without any problem - a rarity in itself. Invariably, if the team comprised very senior officers, the file would be mired in delays, making the visit extremely difficult, mainly because of ego clashes with senior-level bureaucrats. This time, the absence of such friction felt like an unexpected luxury.

Our team consisted of three officers - me, a colleague from the WE Directorate (both of us balanced, forward-thinking souls), and a civilian officer from Directorate General of Quality Assurance (DGQA), who was the human embodiment of suspicion. The man could find conspiracy in a cup of tea!

Now, the thought of visiting Europe gave me such excitement that I had sleepless nights leading up to the trip. Perhaps that's why, on the day of departure in October 2010, I developed a high fever. But did I cancel the trip? Of course not! I did what any self-respecting officer would do - I popped some medicine, got a "fit to fly" certificate from the Base Hospital, and marched on.

We boarded our hopping flight to Prague via Dubai. While my colleagues explored the airport, I curled up in a lounge chair, wrestling with fever, praying to get well soon.

Landing in Prague felt like stepping into a postcard. The crisp morning air, picture-perfect streets, and the promise of adventure were enough to make me forget my fever. Our next stop was Luhacovice, a four-hour road trip away. But what a trip it was! The European countryside rolled past like a live painting - lush meadows, quaint cottages, and roads so smooth that I felt personally offended on behalf of every pothole I'd ever encountered in India.

The official business involved pre-despatch inspection of one engineer equipment, designed to help sappers traverse minefields safely. The equipment had passed all trials, and our job was simple: check, verify, stamp, and leave. Simple, of course, is a relative term, especially when you have a DGQA officer whose default mode is "paranoid."

Despite extensive certifications from legitimate authorities, our DGQA colleague sniffed trouble. After exhausting all logical arguments, we had no choice but to freeze the equipment and demand fresh tests back in India. The manufacturers were baffled. We were frustrated.

With the official work done (or rather undone), we headed to Krakow, Poland. We explored ancient castles steeped in history, where every stone whispered tales from World War II. Then came Vienna, Austria - a city so elegant, it felt like even the street lamps stood straighter out of sheer pride. Clean streets, disciplined traffic, zero pollution, and the sheer respect for pedestrians. It was like stepping into a different world.

Returning to Delhi was... jarring. The area around Army Battle Honours Mess (ABHM), where I stayed temporarily with my wife and two daughters, near Hotel Taj, surrounded by embassies, had always seemed sophisticated and posh. But after Europe? It felt like trying to convince yourself that noodles are gourmet cuisine. The cacophony of honking horns, stray cattle on roads, people treating zebra crossings like abstract art - it was overwhelming.

For the next few days, I looked grim, unusually quiet, and depressed. It was as if I'd left a part of my soul somewhere between Prague's cobblestone streets and Vienna's pristine avenues. My wife noticed the change almost immediately.

"What's wrong with you? Aren't you happy to be back?" she asked, her curiosity morphing into suspicion. Had I developed a 'special friendship' in Europe?

One evening, during our usual walk amidst embassies and chaos, I erupted, "Look at this! No civic sense, traffic rules are optional, people spit wherever they like, and don't even get me started on the pollution. I feel like I need three showers a day!"

She listened patiently, understood why I was depressed all these days, then said with profound wisdom, "Come back to India now. It's where we live."

Just when I thought I had recovered, destiny threw me another surprise - I was sent to the USA the next year for yet another vital equipment for Pangong Tso. The depression was milder this time on return. The reality was sinking in.

After retirement, I travelled extensively across Europe, the Middle East, Southeast Asia, and beyond. Each trip was a revelation, but slowly, acceptance crept in. I realized that India is a beautiful chaos - a land where diversity dances with tradition. Sure, we don't have spotless streets or disciplined drivers, but we have heart, history, and a soul that's uniquely ours.

Now, whenever I hear our PM Modi's vision of making India a developed country by 2047, I smile. Not out of scepticism, but hope. I may not be around to see that dream fully realized, but I pray our future generations will. And maybe, just maybe, they won't have to battle the post-foreign-trip blues like I did.

कुछ तो है इस वतन की मिट्टी में ज़रूर,
जो हर वापसी को घर बना देती है।

SNOW CLEARANCE AND SOARING LAUGHS

In the snow-clad mountains of Manali, heading towards Rohtang and beyond, winter weaves its white magic as early as November. The snow piles up to 10 to 12 feet, burying roads and isolating the region. It's in these harsh conditions that the Border Roads Organisation (BRO) personnel step in, tasked with clearing snow to open lines of communication, and reconnect remote towns and villages. Describing the cold, the blinding white expanses, and the dedication required to operate here barely does justice.

During my tenure as Chief Engineer in BRO from 2013 to 2015, my responsibilities stretched far beyond just the Manali sector. I was in charge of overseeing border infrastructure development across the entire state of Himachal Pradesh and even parts of J&K. The snow-clearing operations in the Manali region, specifically, were managed by one Task Force Commander, who worked directly under me. The Rohtang Tunnel was still under construction, and the roads remained closed for extended periods, leaving the region isolated. However, after the tunnel became operational, the closure times reduced significantly. This story, set before the tunnel's opening, highlights the challenges we faced.

Snow clearing typically began in January, progressing in phases until the roads fully reopened by mid-March. Identifying road alignments beneath the snow was both an art and a skill. As Chief Engineer, I witnessed many such snow-clearing missions, not only in the Manali sector, but other sectors as well, each showcasing extraordinary human perseverance.

But amid the challenges, the Army's ability to find humour in tough situations truly stood out. One such hilarious episode occurred during my first visit to the Manali sector in February 2014 to witness a snow-clearing operation. What was meant to be an official visit soon became an unforgettable adventure filled with snow, skies, and soaring laughter.

Accompanied by my wife and 12 years old daughter, we were excited to not just observe the snow clearing but also indulge in winter sports at Solang Valley - known for skiing, snowboarding, snow scooters, gondola rides, and even paragliding. While I focused on the operations, my wife and daughter had set their sights on ticking paragliding off their bucket list.

At the launch site, we encountered a newlywed couple. The husband, a confident Squadron Leader from the Air Force, stood tall while his petite, nervous wife clung to him, clearly not a fan of adventure.

Before her turn, a hefty tourist was ready to take off. As the operator secured him with the harness, he gave the usual instructions: "Run straight, don't sit until we're airborne, and trust the glide!"

The man sprinted awkwardly towards the edge of the cliff, but gravity had other plans. The paraglider nosedived dramatically, leaving him flailing like an overturned turtle. The crowd erupted in laughter as the man scrambled to his feet, declaring, "I prefer the ground, no interest in the skies!" He stormed off, likely reconsidering his life choices.

Next, it was the turn of the Squadron Leader's wife, who had gone from nervous to terrified after witnessing the previous 'crash landing'. Undeterred, her husband encouraged her: "Come on, sweetheart! It's just like flying in my jet. You'll love it!"

After much cajoling, she reluctantly agreed. She was strapped in, trembling, and as the operator signalled, she shut her eyes, muttered prayers, and began running. Within moments, they were airborne. And that's when the real drama began.

Mid-flight, her fear erupted: "Bachaao! Bachaao! I'm falling! My husband will surely die flying those fighter jets one day, and now he wants me to die too! That's why he pushed me off the cliff! Someone record this - if I don't survive, show this to the police!"

Her shrill cries echoed across the valley, turning heads from paragliders and tourists alike. The Squadron Leader facepalmed while the crowd burst into laughter. The operator, doing his best not to laugh, reassured her mid-flight as they continued. Gradually, her panic subsided, and by the time she landed on snow-covered ground, she was all smiles - embarrassed but exhilarated. She ran to her husband, hugged him, and whispered, "I'm sorry for the drama... but you still pushed me!"

Finally, it was my wife's and daughter's turn. Unfazed by the earlier theatrics, they strapped in confidently, ran, and soared into the sky like pros. Their flawless landings earned applause, and someone commented, "Army families are truly fearless!"

As we concluded our Manali adventure, watching both the mighty snow-clearing operation and the comical spectacles at Solang Valley, I realized that life often throws us into unexpected situations. But it's the laughter, courage, and spirit to embrace the unknown that makes the journey memorable.

मंज़िल उन्हीं को मिलती है, जिन के सपनों में जान होती है।
पंखों से कुछ नहीं होता, हौसलों से उड़ान होती है।

UNPREDICTABLE LANDINGS OF THE CHIEF ENGINEER

Serving in the BRO is not for the chicken-hearted. It's a great mix of Army and General Reserve Engineer Force (GREF) folks, braving the elements in treacherous terrains. Naturally, this creates a unique camaraderie – one that is cemented over landslides, shooting stones, and the shared misery of snowfall.

As the Chief Engineer in BRO from 2013 to 2015, I took my ground visits very seriously. While some officers preferred feedback from their cozy offices, I lived by the golden rule: "One look on the ground is a thousand times better than a briefing in an office."

The only problem? My area of responsibility was vast – stretching across some of the most challenging terrains of the Western Himalayas. Covering it by road was an arduous task, taking 10-15 days to complete a full circuit. The journeys were gruelling, landslide-prone stretches, and unpredictable roadblocks, especially during bad weather and in winters.

Given these challenges, aerial movement became a necessity, especially during winters and when snow-clearance operations were in progress. The Cheetah helicopter allowed me to cover large distances swiftly, ensuring that critical snow-clearance and road-construction operations were monitored in real time. But the unpredictable Himalayan weather had its own plans.

Annadale Helipad in Shimla, my base, was notorious for its bowl-like topography, which frequently trapped clouds, leading to sudden changes in visibility. It was common for me to take off in the early hours under clear skies, only to return in the evening to find Annadale shrouded in mist, making landing impossible. The alternative? A diversion to Chandimandir.

This soon became a routine affair. Anticipating my inevitable diversions, my staff would place a vehicle at both locations whenever I became heliborne. It became something of an inside joke – "Where will the Chief Engineer land today?"

Even officers in my HQ started making bets! Then came the incident that took this whole game to another level.

One day, while I was out on a field visit, my PA received a call from HQ Director General Border Roads (DGBR). A staff officer on the line sounded particularly urgent. "The DGBR wants to speak with the Chief Engineer immediately!" he demanded.

"My apologies, sir," my PA replied in his usual calm demeanour. "The 'Chief' (as they call him in BRO and MES) is on his visit to the Pooh sector and is currently unreachable – possibly mid-air."

"When will he be available?" the officer demanded.

Now, my PA, a cheerful GREF fellow from Uttarakhand, had a knack for humour. Without missing a beat, he responded innocently, "Sir, that's difficult to say. He might land at Annadale, or at Chandimandir... or, who knows, maybe even in Delhi!"

There was silence on the other end. The officer felt a bit offended by such an answer and took it straight to the DGBR. That evening, after finally managing to land in Shimla, I got a call from the DGBR himself.

"Hell of a crazy guy you are!" he chuckled. "Your PA tells no one ever knows where you're going to land! Are you on a mission to enjoy the aerial views from Shimla to Delhi while keeping HQ on their toes?"

I burst into laughter. "Sir, I promise, I'm not enjoying the scenery at government expense. It's just the unpredictable weather keeping things... interesting."

The DGBR laughed again. "Good! I'm very happy that you're regularly visiting your sector, unlike many Chief Engineers who prefer to command from the office."

From then on, my landings – or lack thereof – became a source of entertainment for many. But at the end of the day, every mission was about ensuring that roads were built, passes were cleared, and the men on the ground knew that their 'Chief' was right there with them – whether by road or by air.

ये हवाओं का इत्तेफाक था, या मौसम की ग़ैर यक़ीनी,
चले थे हम अपनी मंजिल की ओर, मगर तक़दीर ने दस्तक तेरे दर पे दी।

OUR FLYING VETERAN AND THE WONKY NECK

If you've ever set foot in Bengal Engineers Group and Centre (BEG & C) Roorkee, you'd know that it's not just any army training establishment - it's a paradise. With its state-of-the-art training infrastructure, an Olympic-sized swimming pool, sprawling sports fields, equestrian facilities, and a magnificent auditorium, the Centre was nothing short of a self-sufficient kingdom. And then, there was the Golf Course, the pride of the station. Even those who had never held a golf club in their lives would find an excuse to amble around its lush green perimeter.

One of the quirkiest landmarks inside the Golf Course was a structure near its entrance, fondly called 'The Wonky Neck'. Decades ago, a storm had bent its umbrella-shaped top, leaving it permanently tilted. Attempts to fix it failed, so it stayed that way - earning its iconic name. Over time, people accepted it, much like they accepted quirky colleagues in the Army who refused to change, no matter what.

In early 2016, while I was the Centre Commandant, a high alert was issued across UP and Uttarakhand. Security was tightened, armed guards manned the gates, entry logs were maintained meticulously, and every vehicle was subjected to thorough check.

Most visitors, including veterans living outside the Centre, complied with the new security regime without much fuss. However, it didn't sit well with one particular retired officer, a freshly minted veteran, who had recently shifted to Roorkee and frequently visited the Centre in his red Tata Manza - mainly for shopping and watching movies at Hajipir Auditorium.

Before the security clampdown, his entry was effortless - just a nod to the sentry and in he went. But now, the ID checks and vehicle searches gnawed at his sense of entitlement. A two-minute inconvenience felt like an insult to him, and he made sure to express his frustration - left, right and centre!

I brushed off complaints about him, thinking he'd eventually adjust, being new to civil life. But he had other ideas.

One fine morning, as the sentry dutifully signalled him to stop, the veteran did the exact opposite - he hit the accelerator and zoomed past the entrance! The guards, caught off guard, were left in a cacophony of frantic whistle blowing. But he was already gone, driving like a fighter pilot on his final mission. One sentry, mistaking it for an actual intrusion, nearly cocked his weapon!

The situation turned serious. With security on high alert, an unidentified speeding vehicle inside the Centre was not to be taken lightly. Through the walkie-talkies, every post was alerted. The red Tata Manza was now officially 'a target of interest'. But our flying veteran didn't stop there. Instead of following the main road, he swerved into the inner lanes, skilfully dodging barriers. And guess where he finally decided to land? Right under the porch of my bungalow - Safar Maina House!

The Adm JCO and a few guards sprinted out, expecting an intruder. Before they could react, the car door swung open, and out he with one friend stepped, completely unfazed, and with an air of authority, declared: "Hi, Kats! Tell these guys to behave. Why the hell do they keep stopping me?"

Suppressing a laugh as I strolled across the lawn, I dismissed the guards and invited him inside. Over tea, I calmly explained, "Sir, given the high alert, security checks are mandatory - even I follow them."

But he was unconvinced. "Come on, I visit the Centre every second day and you know I once served here. The sentries should recognize me by now!" he huffed. "Sentries keep rotating. They can't memorize everyone's face, Sir. Please cooperate." I replied, trying to keep a straight face.

After an hour, he finally left - but the story was far from over. The next day, at the Station Security Conference, attended by all sector commanders, the previous day's incident was the hot topic. Given the widespread discussion, my Deputy Commandant was quick to highlight the issue.

"Gentlemen, we had a security breach yesterday. A vehicle sped past our main gate unchecked. Tomorrow it can happen in any unit. Fortunately, it was not an actual intruder, and the sentry did not open fire. But we need to be extra vigilant. Let's refine our drills to prevent this from happening again."

During the tea break, my Deputy approached me shyly and whispered: "Sir, we've identified the intruder. He claims the Centre Commandant is his regimental officer!" "I know. He crash-landed at my house after his stunt!" I said.

Then, as we were ready to disperse, I added, "You remember that architectural marvel in our Golf Course - the Wonky Neck. Some people are like that structure - no matter how much you try to straighten them, they remain tilted. Instead of fixing them, it's better to guard against them... and enjoy the entertainment they bring!"

ना समझाओ ना बदलने की फ़िक्र करो,
ये निराले लोग ही तो महफ़िल का सुकून हैं।

THE GUEST ROOM GOOF-UP

Roorkee was one of the most satisfying tenures of my 35-year service in the Army. Though it kept me on my toes, I thoroughly enjoyed every bit of it. It was here that I got the privilege of working with the Colonel Commandant, who was a rare combination of clarity, professionalism, and impeccable communication skills.

Before I took over, he had called me over in Delhi and given a simple yet profound directive: "I want all wrong practices in the Centre sorted out as the first priority. I will not interfere in your work, but I will intervene when required."

That one sentence taught me the fine distinction between interfering and intervening. His wisdom and strategic leadership made my tenure not just memorable but also a great learning experience. His wife, a dignified and candid lady, was equally mature, and my wife held her in great regard.

Roorkee, being a gateway to various pilgrimage destinations in Uttarakhand, was always abuzz with visitors - senior officers, veterans, and their families. The annual Group Day Celebrations was the grandest of all events, blending formal discussions, intense deliberations, and lively social functions.

Nov 2016: Two days, out of three days of Group Day events, saw the Colonel Commandant chairing a conference where unit commanders presented their reports. The key Centre appointments shared the latest policies, and finally, the Colonel Commandant gave his overall perspective and directions aiming at improving the overall operational efficiency of the units and strengthening the legacy of the Bengal Sappers. The veterans, side by side, were given a tour of the Centre, giving them a glimpse into various improvements, and the ladies engaged in welfare activities and social events. With so much happening, my wife and I barely had time for a conversation.

On one such busy day, the ladies were in the middle of their Ladies Meet. My wife was seated next to the Colonel Commandant's wife, enjoying the performances put up by the Centre's ladies.

"Sapna," she said casually, "I see many improvements since you and your husband took over. The Centre looks wonderful! Even the guest rooms have been done up nicely. But you know, Abbey, the Number 1 Guest Room needs a makeover. It should be worthy of VIPs."

My wife took this comment in stride, happy that our efforts were being recognized.

Meanwhile, I was in a parallel world, attending the conference with the unit commanders. After the session, the officers gathered for a light-hearted lunch at the venue where the Ladies Meet was being held, and the conversation soon drifted to further improvements at the Centre.

I, completely unaware of what had transpired in the Ladies Meet, casually remarked: "Sir, I have stayed in the guest rooms at HQ DGBR Officers' Mess multiple times when I was the Chief Engineer in BRO. Honestly, they need serious revamping - the décor is outdated, and the food quality is horrible. They're not quite up to the mark for senior officers."

The Colonel Commandant nodded in agreement. But his wife? She suddenly became strangely quiet. My wife, who was sitting next to her, looked alarmed.

That evening, as we returned to Safar Maina House, the much-envied abode of the Centre Commandant, my wife, visibly upset, confronted me. "Why on earth did you bring up the DGBR guest rooms issue?" she demanded. Still clueless, I replied, "It was a casual chat. What's the big deal?"

Then she dropped the bombshell: "In the morning, the Colonel Commandant's wife had suggested revamping Abbey. Now, it looks like I passed that information to you, and you raised it with her husband, almost as if to counter her suggestion."

For a moment, I felt the ground slip beneath my feet. What an uncanny coincidence! How could I have known what had transpired between the ladies? It now appeared as though my wife and I had devised a strategy to challenge her suggestion.

The evening Officers' Mess party went on grandly, but I noticed the Colonel Commandant's wife maintaining a subtle distance. My wife, equally unnerved, seemed withdrawn, and I felt a pang of guilt.

The next day after the brunch, we went to Abbey to see off the Colonel Commandant and his wife. Over a cup of coffee, she finally voiced what perhaps had been bothering her. Looking at me, she said in a low voice, "It looks like my suggestion to renovate Abbey wasn't taken well by you. That's why you brought up guest room improvements at DGBR to my husband, isn't it?"

I wasted no time in clearing the misunderstanding. I explained how it was a sheer coincidence - completely unplanned and unintentional. To my relief, she accepted my explanation.

Despite the resolution, my wife could sense that the warmth in her interactions with the Colonel Commandant's wife was slightly diminished. Things weren't quite the same for some time.

Determined to set things right, I took immediate action. I instructed my Mess Secretary to renovate Abbey with contemporary design elements, fresh furniture, and upholstery. The entire project was completed in just three months.

Soon after, the Colonel Commandant, now elevated to E-in-C, visited the Centre again. This time, he and his wife were hosted in the newly renovated Abbey. On seeing it, both were visibly stunned. His wife finally smiled and said with her husband, almost together, "Now, this looks like a VIP guest room!"

We all laughed, and with that, the last traces of the misunderstanding vanished.

In hindsight, it was a light hearted mix-up, but it reaffirmed an important lesson - maturity, understanding, and timely communication can prevent misunderstandings from escalating.

विलादत होता है जो संगीन दरार-ए-रिश्ता, गलतफहमी से अक्सर,
रंजिशे मिट जाती हैं वहीं, हकीकत के अज़्म से।

TEE-RRIFIC TALE OF THE MISSING NAME FROM THE TEE BOARD

When I assumed the role of Centre Commandant at Roorkee in November 2015, the time was ripe for transformation. From training to infrastructure, administration to sports, everything was getting a much-needed revamp. But one area that stood out as particularly ripe for improvement was the golf course - Three Feathers Golf Course (later renamed AEPTA). It was a charming little spot, perfect for a leisurely round, but it needed a makeover.

My first project was to commission a grand structure near the Golf Hut: a towering monument in the shape of a giant ball resting on a tee, to adore the entrance of the course. Along with that, we enhanced the course's playability - fine-tuning the greens and reshaping the fairways.

Then, an idea struck me like a bolt of lightning: What if we added a 'Tee Board' at each hole? Not just any board, but one that would display the name of the previous Centre Commandant, a brief mention of their contributions to the course, and details like the hole number, distance, par, stroke index, and layout. I pitched the idea to the Golf Secretary and other golfers, and it was an instant hit!

The beauty of the idea was that all the work was handled by tradesmen undergoing training at the Centre. The Ball-and-Tee structure went up first, followed by the Pro Shop, designed to complement the overall ambiance. As for the Tee Boards, they were a labour of love. Each board required thoughtful research, capturing the personalities of past commandants and succinctly summarizing their legacies in a few lines. It was a painstaking process, but the team worked tirelessly, and the results were worth every ounce of effort.

The first thing any golfer noticed upon entering the course was the towering Ball-and-Tee structure, standing about eight feet tall and perfectly placed to capture the attention. As they teed off, their eyes would quickly be drawn to the Tee Boards at each hole. These boards were so distinctive that golfers often paused to read the tribute to the commandant after whom the hole was named, admiring the innovative concept. It was a novelty that was unlike anything they had seen before.

But as with any good story, there was a twist. One day, a former Centre Commandant visited the Centre. After playing a round, he noticed something odd at Hole Number 9 - his name was on the Tee Board, along with a brief description of his contributions. Furious, he stormed, "Who put my name here? I wasn't ever asked - this is unacceptable!"

His annoyance reached me, and I was taken aback. Everyone else had praised the boards, yet here he was, furious about being mentioned without his consent. Without missing a beat, I ordered, "Remove his name and everything written about him on the Tee Board. But leave the rest intact."

Fast forward to the Centre's biannual celebrations - a three-day event attended by ex-centre commandants, senior officers, and esteemed guests. One of the highlights was, of course, the round of golf. As expected, the Tee Boards received high praise. But when we reached Hole Number 9, one senior officer remarked, "Kats, this is a remarkable idea. But why does the board here lack the name of the commandant? It's quite strange."

I felt a wave of discomfort, unsure how to explain the situation without causing a scene. Fortunately, the mystery was soon unravelled. It turned out that the commandant in question had taken offense at his name being displayed without prior approval, prompting me to have it removed. The revelation sent ripples through the crowd, and one officer quipped, "He's known for his quirky behaviour. He should've been more sporting about it." Laughter followed, and we moved on, but the mystery of Hole Number 9 lingered.

Over time, the incident became a running joke. Whenever a visitor played at the Centre, they'd ask about the missing name on Hole Number 9. The locals, always ready with a wink, would reveal the tale behind it, which was met with a mix of ridicule and amusement.

In April 2018, after completing my two-and-a-half-year tenure, I moved on from the Centre. I didn't attend any Group Day celebrations until 2023. When I returned to play during one reunion, something caught my eye: the improvements were still in place - the Ball-and-Tee structure, the Pro Shop, the Tee Boards - but Hole Number 9 had a surprise. The name of that same former Centre Commandant, removed years earlier, was back on the board!

Curious, I asked one of the old-timers about it, and he told me, "After years of ridicule, he realized that the hole without his name was more conspicuous than having it there. So, he asked the Centre to put his name back, hoping the mystery would finally fade away."

It seemed the ego had been subdued, and a lesson learnt: sometimes, it's better to embrace the tribute than let pride stand in the way.

गुरुर को ख़ाक में मिला कर इंसान ने सीखा,
जो कभी न था वही अब सबसे प्यारा लगने लगा।

THE GREAT GOLF GAMBIT : A GAME OF SWINGS AND SCHEMES

It was early November 2015 when I landed in Roorkee as the Commandant of the BEG & C - a position so coveted that only a few in an entire course get the privilege to hold it. Commandant, often called 'mai-baap', was responsible for everything - training, administration, welfare, and ensuring that over 5,000 soldiers present in the Centre didn't turn the place into a chaotic mela. If anything went wrong, I knew exactly where the buck stopped, ofcourse on my desk.

From Day One, I got down to business, cracking the whip on reforms, training innovations, and welfare projects. My team and I left no stone unturned. Soon, visitors and trainees alike started noticing the change. Even higher HQ took note and showered us with compliments. But as they say, life is never a smooth fairway - there's always a bunker waiting.

The newly appointed GOC of the Uttar Bharat Area was scheduled for a two-day visit. His reputation preceded him - a man of unwavering certitude, convinced of his own infallibility, and known for assigning peculiar, often inscrutable tasks. Yet, he had been well-briefed by his staff at Bareilly about our accomplishments.

His two-day visit kicked off with a detailed presentation, followed by a windshield tour of the Centre. I could tell he was impressed, though he wasn't one to openly admit it. That evening, we hosted him for a full-course continental dinner with the traditional military fanfare - pipe bands, polished silver trophies, and all. He was visibly won over, leaving behind one of the finest remarks in the visitor book.

Then came Day Two - the real test.

The GOC, an avid albeit middling golfer, had played since his academy days. More importantly, he was a lamentable loser. A discreet warning had been whispered to us: "Let him win, or there will be ramifications."

As we teed off, everything seemed fine. For the first nine holes, my partner and I had the upper hand. The GOC, however, started showing signs of distress. He became anxious, his shots went haywire, and the more he tried, the worse it got.

After the ninth hole, over a lavish breakfast at the Golf Hut, I muttered to my partner, "This doesn't seem to be the GOC's day. Perhaps we should feign some ineptitude?"

Feign, we did! I even botched a two-foot putt, deliberately taking three strokes. Yet, fate had conspired otherwise - despite our most concerted efforts to let him win, we still emerged victorious. The GOC looked visibly unhappy.

More than him, though, it was me and my team who were perplexed - our well-intended plan had backfired spectacularly.

As we shook hands at the end, the GOC, forcing a smile, said, "We'll soon have a revenge round. This time at Bareilly. Let's see how you win there?"

The visit continued with one inauguration and a training demonstration, and by the time the GOC left, he was impressed with the Centre but carried the hidden pain of his golf defeat.

A few days later, curiosity got the better of me, and I called his staff officer for feedback. "The GOC was very happy with the visit," he reported. "But what have you done to him? He's spending more time on the golf course than in his office!"

I mused for a moment. Clearly, losing was not part of his grand strategy. But what happened next left me even more convinced. One morning, my Superintendent of Training (ST) walked into my office, holding a letter from the Area HQ. "Sir, we've been asked to submit a paper on 'Oversight of Regimental Centres'... in 15 days."

I nearly spilled my tea. A research paper? This was his way of getting back at us for denting his ego on the golf course!

For the next 15 days, my team and I were buried under paperwork, gathering inputs from other Centres, speaking to seniors, and burning the midnight oil. No golf at all. Providence, however, had its own idiosyncratic sense of justice. When the next conference at Bareilly was held, I happened to be on leave. My Deputy attended in my absence. And guess what? No golf was played.

Our victory from Roorkee remained untouched. The GOC never got his counter-round, but we certainly got an unforgettable memory - a simple golf game that led to 15 days of research, revenge, and regret.

नज़रें थीं निशाने पर तक़दीर दगा दे गई,
इक छोटी सी शिकस्त दिल पर खला दे गई।

SPEAK UP OR PERISH : A LESSON IN LEADERSHIP

"You should be seen and not heard." That's the first commandment for a YO joining an Army unit. The idea is simple - absorb, learn, and master the fundamentals before forming opinions. And so, in every unit, freshers are groomed under this doctrine.

Some take it seriously and flourish. But a few take it so literally that even after growing up, they continue to toe the seniors' line, never voicing their own thoughts. That wasn't going to be my story.

When I joined, I was naturally reserved. My Company Commander, a thorough professional, kept me on my toes, ensuring I learnt every nuance of soldiering. Under his watchful eyes, I was groomed well. But as years passed, a senior once remarked, "If you don't speak up now, when the hell will you?" That struck a chord.

Gradually, I learnt not just to form my own thoughts but to express them with conviction. As I climbed the ranks, I ensured my opinions were well-considered and carefully articulated. And people listened. But not everyone appreciated it - some feared being overshadowed.

After two demanding tenures in flag rank, I was posted as Chief Engineer of the largest pivot Corps. It was a mammoth responsibility - numerous engineer units under my jurisdiction and operational works spread over 10-odd military stations. I was busy, to say the least. Then came the call from the Technical Secretary (TS) to the E-in-C. "Sir, we need a two-day itinerary for the E-in-C's visit. Please send it as soon as possible."

I prepared the draft and informed my senior engineer officer at the Command HQ about the broad plan. His reaction: "Why wasn't I informed of this visit?"

"I don't know, Sir, but the TS is pressing for the itinerary."

A proud Bengal Sapper like me, he was a hard taskmaster - genial with seniors but quick-tempered with subordinates. I shared the draft, expecting a response. A day passed, silence. The TS kept chasing me. So, after waiting long enough, I sent the itinerary directly.

The E-in-C's visit went smoothly. He was thoroughly briefed, praised the engineers, and enjoyed dinner at the Corps Commander's residence. Everything had gone well.

The very next day, as I relaxed with a guest in my lawn, my phone rang. The voice on the other end was incensed. "Why the hell did you send the itinerary without my approval?"

I was taken aback but calmly reminded him that I had shared the draft first and received no feedback. His response was a furious outburst, loud enough for my guest to overhear. Then, with a final "I don't mollycoddle people, even if they're from my own regiment!" he banged the phone. I felt insulted but let it pass.

A few days later, a letter arrived: "A brainstorming session is scheduled to discuss the restructuring of engineer units for the new concept of warfighting. All Chief Engineers and one CO from each formation to attend."

He had already worked out his restructuring proposal. This meeting was just a rubber-stamping exercise. At the session, he eloquently explained his well-researched plan with strategic insight.

One by one, the officers took turns praising the plan, tweaking it just enough to sound involved. But no real critique. What was supposed to be a brainstorming session had turned into a chorus of admiration.

I sat silently, observing the spectacle. Finally, he turned to me. "Kataria, you've been awfully quiet. Let's hear your thoughts."

The moment had come. "Sir, your proposal is well-structured but has serious inadequacies. It is likely to break the basic cohesiveness of sub-units, badly disrupt their homogeneity, and impact command & control, thus reducing their operational effectiveness."

I backed my statement with clear examples. A deep silence fell over the Conference Room. His face hardened, the colour changing visibly. "Thanks, Kataria. We will consider your points," his voice, measured.

Post-session, during high tea, the usual chatter was absent. People avoided eye contact as if an unspoken taboo had been broken. Then, as he shook hands with everyone, he turned to me. "Let's meet in my office before you leave."

I entered his office, expecting another rebuke. But instead, his demeanour had transformed. He offered me coffee.

"How's everything up in Jodhpur? Your GOC speaks highly of you. That water conservation paper for the Military Station you submitted there - please share a copy with me."

His tone had softened. He had realized his overreaction, received a positive report about my performance, and most importantly, witnessed my ability to challenge ideas with reason.

Shortly after, I was posted to a new, more demanding role as Chief Engineer in the MES. But this episode remained a testament to one truth: There's a time to stay silent and learn. And then there's a time to speak up. And when that time comes, one must not falter.

बड़ी बेरौनकी है ये महफ़िल,
हर तरफ़ ख़ुशामदी का आलम है,
एक ही कलाम सुनाई देता है यहाँ,
और लोग इसे तबादला-ए-ख़्याल कहते हैं!

THE GOC'S FAREWELL FORE

My early years in the regiment ingrained a simple yet profound lesson: self-respect and principles are non-negotiable while everything else can be adjusted. I took this quite literally and have tried to live by it ever since.

Jodhpur, 2018 to 2019 - As the Chief Engineer of the largest pivot Corps, my responsibilities were immense. With numerous engineer units under my jurisdiction and overseeing high security operational works at multiple military stations, kept me fully occupied. But amidst these duties, I had another role - Golf Captain - which often brought its own share of amusement.

The COS was a professional to the core, disciplined, meticulous, a man of few words and a passionate golfer. In contrast, the GOC was a different breed altogether - flamboyant, entitled, and excessively conscious of his stature. He thrived on elaborate protocols, expecting nothing less than regal treatment and the world to orbit around him. His love for golf, though prominently listed in his biodata, was mostly theoretical. When he did step onto the Course, his enthusiasm far outweighed his skill. Golfers often joked that he would have fared better on the hockey field than on the greens.

As his tenure drew to a close, a grand farewell was meticulously planned under the watchful eye of COS. Every minute detail was submitted for the GOC's approval - his word was gospel, after all. My role was to plan and execute the Golfing Out ceremony, ensuring a smooth transition by welcoming the new GOC alongside bidding farewell to the outgoing one.

The event was structured to perfection - a round of golf, a prize distribution ceremony, a farewell speech, and a grand lunch at the Golf Course. Both GOCs and their spouses participated, with station officers joining in to showcase camaraderie. The prize distribution was thoughtfully divided between both of them and their wives, maintaining a fine balance.

Everything unfolded like clockwork. The event was a resounding success, earning widespread appreciation. Yet, something was amiss. The GOC seemed oddly unsettled avoiding eye contact, scanning the crowd restlessly, and barely touching his lunch. For a man who demanded attention, his unusual silence stood out.

I sensed something was brewing but brushed aside this thought - after all, the event had gone exactly as planned, and as approved by the GOC.

The next morning, an early call from COS, "Kats, we need to meet the GOC in his office, first thing in the morning". It felt bizarre ... why a meeting so soon after a successful event?

When I arrived, COS was already there, standing uncharacteristically muted. The GOC, instead of his usual formality, got straight to the point, his tone thunderous. "I AM STILL THE GOC, even if my successor is in the station. Yesterday's event was NOT conducted the way I WANTED!"

Walking back, I turned to COS, expecting some clarity. His smirk suggested he had seen this coming.

It wasn't a major lapse - just the GOC's way of asserting control one last time. Perhaps he had envisioned a different format, such as playing with a single club, an eccentric idea he had floated before. Or maybe he wanted full control over the prize distribution, excluding any involvement from his successor and his wife.

The paradox was hard to miss. Every detail had been put up for his approval, signed off by him. Yet, here we were, deciphering his displeasure like an unsolvable riddle. For a moment, I wondered if he truly believed golf could be played with a single club. But then again, that wasn't golf, it was hockey!

A few days later, at the formal farewell, all officers lined up to shake hands with the GOC, wishing him well for his next posting.

As he moved down the line shaking hands with everyone, he reached me. He extended his hand for a handshake, I did not extend mine. Instead, I looked him in the eye and said, "Thank you for everything, sir. All the best."

His hand remained mid-air for a brief second before he awkwardly withdrew it. The message was clear - for people like him, self respect might be optional, but for self respecting professionals like us, it was everything. And so, with a silent farewell and an unshaken hand, I walked away. Not out of defiance, but with the quiet dignity of someone who understood the true value of self esteem.

Ironically, some years later, while playing at Shivalik Environmental Park & Training Area (SEPTA) Chandimandir, I met his course mate. With a wry smile, he remarked, "You know, that chap leads a solitary life now, hardly anyone interacts with him." I wasn't surprised. After all, I had seen it coming.

तमन्ना जो की बुलंदी की छोड़ दामन अपनो का,
भरी महफ़िल में भी अब बेगानों सा फिरता हूँ मैं।

LOVE LETTERS, LEADERSHIP AND LESSONS FROM MES

The Army War College at Mhow is where leadership theories collide with the harsh realities of command. As a DS, I taught management capsules also to future commanders, covering leadership styles - transformational versus transactional, and democratic versus autocratic.

Student officers, brimming with theoretical confidence, debated leadership concepts with the kind of conviction that could've made even Sun Tzu reconsider his strategies. But real-life case studies could humble them, revealing that leadership isn't about flexing authority - it's about adapting, understanding and occasionally writing what I fondly call 'love letters.' But more on that later.

After braving the relentless heat of Jodhpur, I landed in Srinagar in June 2018 as the Chief Engineer in MES, trading scorching deserts for the chill of the valley. Little did I know, the climate wasn't the only contrast - I was stepping into a command environment far more complex than temperature shifts.

The MES is a unique organisation - a mixed-cadre setup of civilian and Army personnel. Its structure comes with its own set of command challenges and peculiarities, demanding not just leadership but intelligent and mature management. Unlike traditional army units, MES doesn't respond well to rigid thinking. It thrives on reasoning, mutual respect and adaptability.

I had barely started my familiarisation tour when the government threw a curveball - Article 370's revocation. Like an unexpected grenade at a tea party, it blew up every plan.

Communication lines collapsed, the internet vanished, and migrant labour disappeared. My MES works? Frozen solid.

But MES is fuelled by grit. While civilians struggled, my station teams went into commando mode - fetching even maintenance stores from Jammu, dodging curfews, and using their own transport.

Just as things started to stabilize, COVID-19 arrived, slamming the world into a total clampdown. Civilian staff vanished, but our men in uniform held the line - manning substations, pumping stations, and essential services. While civil areas floundered, MES ensured military stations remained functional. The Corps Commander embodied a unique combination - a result-oriented infantry officer with an autocratic streak. His attention to detail and commitment to operational excellence were undeniable. However, his leadership style left little room for free dialogue, often leading to lower formation commanders dancing to his tunes, a familiar scenario in any organisational culture.

One day, one senior staff officer from Corps HQ called, sounding like he'd rather be anywhere else. "Sir, the GOC wants to see you. Some station commanders have raised complaints about MES maintenance services." Ah, the age-old tradition - when in doubt, blame MES, the Army's soft punching bag.

The next day, I entered the GOC's office. He wasted no time. "Kats, MES works are in a shambles. Essential services disrupted. What's happening?" I replied, "Sir, perhaps the station commanders can present their observations at tomorrow's works conference. We'll address them point by point. It's ironic that a one-hour power cut often overshadows the comfort of the other 23 hours of uninterrupted supply."

That response didn't go down well. While the staff officer looked like he wanted to disappear, the GOC snapped, "Send love letters to all your Commander Works Engineers (CWE), copy to me."

I drafted them my way, knowing the ground realities: "I commend the efforts of your GEs under tough conditions. However, pending maintenance contracts are a concern. While station commanders now hold responsibility, let's double our efforts, guide them proactively, and put our shoulders to the yoke in steering the issue forward."

The GOC wasn't amused. When I was summoned again, he smirked. "Kats, is this how love letters are written? They read more like award citations. Shall I give you one to show how it's done?!"

I smiled. "Sir, I believe appreciation motivates better than admonishment under the circumstances." A rare, almost human smile crossed his face. "Fair enough. Carry on."

As I pen this story, I can't help but say - if leadership is an art, then the MES is the perfect canvas, where even the boldest strokes need a little shading. And when it comes to love letters, a dash of sweetness often does the trick better than a sledgehammer. After all, it's much easier to fix a leaky tap than to mend a bruised ego!

Had I been the DS now, this would've been an interesting case study, sparking debates on which leadership style - transformational, transactional, democratic or autocratic - would be most suited to the MES under such conditions.

दिल ही तो है न संग-ओ-ख़िश्त, दर्द से भर न आए क्यों,
रोएँगे हम हज़ार बार, कोई हमें सताए क्यों?

THE TIGER'S PANDEMIC MARCH

In the Army, the head of any establishment is often called the 'Tiger'. Every unit and formation has one. As a YO, I often wondered whether these bosses truly possessed animal instincts or if the title was just a confidence booster. Over time, I realized it worked like a magic spell. Some began to believe the world revolved around them, their word was final, and even nature had to seek their approval before making a move.

During my tenure as Chief Engineer in the MES at Srinagar, I encountered two such Tigers, each with his own quirks and completely opposite characteristics. The first left soon after the purge of Article 370, perhaps breathing a sigh of relief, narrowly escaping the storm that was to follow. Then, in January 2020, the new GOC arrived - a man of humility who quite coincidentally, brought COVID-19 along as his invisible sidekick. I sometimes imagine the previous Tiger sipping coffee somewhere, thanking his stars for dodging this double whammy.

By March 2020, Badami Bagh Cantonment was frozen in time. The lockdown was so strict that even shadows seemed hesitant to move. Infrastructure projects stalled, movements halted, and the cantonment transformed into a ghost town. People stayed locked indoors as if the Corona virus lurked in the corridors, ready to pounce. Windows shut, conversations vanished, and even the bravest officers suddenly discovered a newfound passion for housekeeping.

Then came Lockdown 2.0 with even harsher restrictions. Stepping out was forbidden unless absolutely necessary. Just when we thought things couldn't get worse, Tiger had an epiphany. One fine evening, he issued an order that left everyone stunned.

"Why are we cowering inside our homes? When restrictions eased after Lockdown 1.0, hardly anyone fell seriously ill. It's just a mild infection! I want all officers to step out and walk with me around the station. We shall set an example!"

Had this been an ordinary directive, there would have been the usual grumbles followed by reluctant compliance. But this was Lockdown 2.0, and stepping outside felt like testing fate. Panic spread. Was this about boosting morale or simply defying common sense? Despite all apprehensions, around 20 officers, including me and the 'Navratnas', gathered at the designated spot. And what a sight we were - masked, gloved, clad in tracksuits, caps pulled low, some even wearing sunglasses to cover every exposed inch. The result? Nobody could recognize anybody. Even the Tiger struggled to identify his herd.

Our unintended formation added to the hilarity. Maintaining exaggerated social distance, we spread across the road like a marching band that had forgotten its own tune. Our slow, synchronized steps, each man cautiously following the other, resembled a flock of ducks waddling around the SEPTA pond, each pretending to be braver than the one ahead.

The walk began in complete silence, with no casual chatter, just the rhythmic sound of footsteps. Under normal circumstances, we would have occupied a much smaller stretch of road. But that day, our march stretched far beyond visible distance. Officers at the rear had no clue whether the group was still walking or had disappeared into the mist.

An hour into this surreal stroll, one Navratna whispered from a very safe distance to the ADC, "What exactly was the purpose of this?"

The ADC replied just as cautiously, "To motivate the station, apparently. Fresh air never hurt anyone, just follow safety rules!"

Whether the station felt motivated or mortified, nobody knows. But rumour has it that Command HQ got wind of this historic march, and their reaction wasn't exactly applause. Soon after, the walks vanished into oblivion. Lockdown 2.0 was back in full force, with strict adherence re-imposed.

As for our fearless Tiger, he remained unseen outside his den for several days. Perhaps he was busy strategizing his next grand campaign - his beloved station cleanliness drive. Or maybe, he had simply realized that some battles are best fought from the safety of indoors.

तेरे इश्क़ की रानाई ने क्या-क्या न करवाया मुझसे,
लोग उसको भूल मुझको ही दीवाना कहने लगे।

<u>THE ART OF KNOWING WHEN TO STOP</u>

In higher HQ, it's rare to find the boss and his deputy pulling in perfect harmony. More often than not, there's a silent tug of war, if not an outright clash. Friction might not always be visible, but it bubbles under the surface, showing up in subtle ways.

After completing three tenures in flag rank, I landed in Srinagar in 2019 as the Zonal Chief Engineer, the senior-most in my formation after the GOC. The pressure was immense, especially after the abrogation of Article 370. A short working season, a dwindling contractor base, paucity of migrant labour, delay in construction material fetching up from below - it felt like juggling flaming torches while riding a unicycle. But I had an ace up my sleeve: the new GOC, a sharp, pragmatic officer and an old course mate from Staff College. He understood the ground realities and appreciated the technical expertise my office provided. My advice was welcomed, and decisions flowed smoothly, creating an oddly satisfying professional rhythm.

Life was good - until a new COS arrived. Freshly promoted, much junior to me, and radiating the confidence of someone who had once, a decade ago, handled MES works as a staff officer in a static, non-fighting formation HQ. That experience had apparently turned him into an overnight infrastructure guru - or so he believed.

In our very first meeting, he announced, "Sir, one day we'll walk up to the new Corps HQ building under construction. I have ideas to make it even better."

A few days later, I found myself accompanying him to the construction site, with another senior staff officer dealing with works from his HQ. The project superstructure was nearly complete - a modern, three-story marvel blending heritage with contemporary design. Five years of meticulous planning and hard work seeking necessary approvals had culminated in a structure that was to stand proud and dignified.

But the COS had his mental toolbox ready. "Why can't we have central cooling and heating?" "The windows look so small, let's make them bigger and replace their frames with UPVC!" "And additional toilets - can't we squeeze in a few more?" Likewise, many more wild suggestions...

I blinked, wondering if he'd accidentally time-travelled from the project's conceptual phase. Air conditioning in Srinagar? Additional toilets after the plumbing was nearly done? Bigger windows, ignoring the architectural aesthetics and energy efficiency despite optimized lighting? My internal monologue was having a fun day, but outwardly, I stayed composed.

"Sir," I replied politely, "I'll examine all these points, discuss them with my team, and present our recommendations to the GOC - in your presence, of course."

Fast forward a week. Armed with a detailed PowerPoint presentation, my team and I laid out each of his suggestions, highlighting technical challenges, implications in terms of cost and time overrun, and the minor issue of potentially having to demolish parts of the building to implement them. Not to mention the approvals needed from the ministry, which could stretch longer than the construction itself.

I concluded with a simple remark: "Sir, the MES can build even the Taj Mahal if you wish, but the right approvals must be in place at the right time."

The GOC, sharp as ever, absorbed the presentation quietly and finally remarked, "Let's stick to the approved design. The old timers were knowledgeable too."

I thought the matter was settled. Oh, how naive I was!

The officer, undeterred by minor setbacks like logic and feasibility, saw a new opportunity when the E-in-C planned a visit to the formation. This, he decided, was his moment. During the site inspection, while the E-in-C was being briefed by my team, the officer sprang into action, tossing out the same suggestions like confetti.

The E-in-C, a highly seasoned customer in MES works, listened patiently. Then, with an expression betraying nothing, he turned to me and said, "What's the problem, Kats? Do what he says."

I started to explain the technical constraints, but something was off. There was a glint in his eye, a subtle wink that no one else noticed. The message was clear - Play along...

So, every time the officer suggested another impractical modification, the E-in-C repeated, "Kats, I already told you - do what he says," followed by another discreet wink.

The officer was ecstatic; convinced he had secured the green light for all his visionary changes. He wasted no time instructing his staff officer to draft detailed notes of the visit, outlining the decisions he believed had been endorsed. Several iterations to the draft, and self-congratulatory nods later, the document was despatched to the E-in-C's branch.

Weeks passed. The officer kept pestering me to start implementing the changes. I politely suggested, "Let's wait for the official tour notes."

Two months later, the much anticipated tour notes finally arrived. They were brief, almost poetic in their simplicity: "The E-in-C visited various ongoing MES works. He appreciated the quality and progress. Regarding the new Corps HQ building, he was impressed with the integration of heritage and modern design. It is imperative that the pace of work continues without deviation from laid-down MES procedures." .

No mention of central cooling. No bigger windows. No surprise toilets. Just a polite nod to sticking with the original plan.

The COS was shell-shocked. Rumour has it he even scolded his staff officer, though for what, no one knew! When the GOC read the notes, he simply smiled. Not because of any hidden victory, but because the E-in-C's working style was an art form - a masterclass in diplomacy wrapped in cryptic efficiency.

In the end, the lesson was simple: You can't be a jack of all trades. Respect the professionals. Trust the process. And sometimes, old timers knew exactly what they were doing.

वो सोचते रहे बदलेंगे कायनात को,
हम मुस्कराए और वक्त के साथ चल दिए।

POSTING ROULETTE : SPIN THE MS WHEEL

If there's one branch in the Army that could put top magicians to shame, it's the ever enigmatic MS Branch - fondly (and sometimes not-so-fondly) known by its legendary acronym 'Mysteries & Surprises'. True to its name, this branch has a knack for turning simple requests into complex puzzles, keeping officers perpetually on their toes - geographically, emotionally, and sometimes even philosophically.

I remember overhearing a wise old officer chuckle once, "You ask for East, they'll send you West. You dream of a peace station, and voilà - welcome to a hard field posting!" I thought it was just a casual chatter until life decided to serve me a firsthand experience.

Take, for example, one good friend of mine. At the fag end of his service, he requested a compassionate ground posting to his home station in Banglore. The MS Branch, with the calm of a saint and the precision of a surgeon, nodded thoughtfully... and posted him to Kolkata. Their reasoning? "Kolkata is an equally good peace station. And whatever you need from Bangalore can easily be managed from Kolkata."

Ah, the logic of the MS Branch - undeniable, unchallengeable, and as smooth as a freshly pressed uniform on GOC's conference day.

Early in my career, a third-generation senior officer, clearly scarred by his own trysts with the MS, offered me a nugget of wisdom: "Never ask for a posting. The moment you do, the MS Branch treats it like a suggestion box entry - acknowledged with a polite nod, then promptly ignored."

For over three decades, I followed this advice with utmost discipline. Whenever the ritual letter arrived: "You are under consideration for your next posting. Please exercise your option so that your posting aligns with your aspirations," I'd smile, fold it neatly, and let destiny work its magic.

But then came the day when my wife decided to challenge the system while we were at Jodhpur. "Why don't you ask for your choice this time? You never know, you might just get it!" she urged with the conviction of someone who's never dealt with the MS Branch. "How innocent you are!" I thought, amused. But after years of tactical dodging, I finally surrendered.

With a heart full of hope and a dash of scepticism, I penned down my modest, heartfelt request: Ambala Cantt. Simple, practical - close to home, good for our daughter's college plans, and perfect for settling down.

A month later, the MS Branch responded. My posting order read: "Chief Engineer, Srinagar Zone."

I held the letter up like it was the punchline of a cosmic joke. "You insisted, now face the music!" I grinned at my wife, whose face could've easily launched a thousand sarcastic remarks.

Off we went to Srinagar, convinced this was my final posting - the grand finale of a colourful career. But the MS Branch wasn't done with its twists.

About seven months before I hung my boots, I got the inevitable call: "Be ready to be posted out." "But... why? You told me Srinagar was my last stop!" "Ah, as per policy (don't we all love that phrase?), you cannot retire from an executive appointment. We'll give you an easy staff posting now."

An easy staff posting? I braced myself, half-expecting to be despatched to a forgotten corner of the North-East, a place untouched by me during my service. And then, like the final twist in a Bollywood plot, my posting order arrived: Chandimandir, Command HQ.

Now here's the kicker - our flat in Mohali was waiting to be renovated. My daughter's postgraduate plans? Perfectly aligned. My wife's reaction? Let's just say if joy had a volume knob, hers was cranked up to full blast.

Those last few months were a breeze. I renovated our flat, helped my daughter with her post-graduation choice, and even enjoyed my full quota of leave - a luxury I'd never experienced before.

Looking back, I realize the MS Branch wasn't just dishing out random postings. Whether knowingly or unknowingly, driven by the diktat of my destiny, they were guiding me exactly where I needed to be. Every twist, every surprise, and every "in the interest of the organization" justification played its part in the larger script.

And in the end, what did I learn? That trusting the journey often leads you to destinations far better than the ones you'd planned. Srinagar, after all, turned out to be a slice of paradise, a place my wife had dreamt of visiting first post-retirement. Destiny just gave her an extended preview, courtesy our great Army.

ख़ुदी को कर बुलंद इतना कि हर तक़दीर से पहले,
ख़ुदा बंदे से ख़ुद पूछे बता तेरी रज़ा क्या है?

BUGGY RIDES AND VANISHING TRADITIONS

It was the final chapter of my 35-year service, my last posting before I hung up my boots. Landing in Chandimandir from Srinagar on a staff appointment, I found myself not battling red tape or privileges for the patrician few but quietly contemplating what was sacred and what had degenerated into mere formalities. It was about tradition, once held dear, now dissolving into the fog of convenience and indifference.

When I was commissioned at the IMA, we were imbued with this tenet that "an officer is an officer irrespective of his rank and must always be treated as such." This axiom was accentuated at BEG & C Roorkee before heading for the YO's course at CME. The officers' mess had a simple, unwavering tradition - every YO was ceremoniously dined in, a memory etched forever with the classic ritual of getting their backsides blessed with paper canes and downing the infamous 'Sapper Punch' in one go. The climax? Standing before the Commandant, introducing oneself with gusto, "Sir, I am so-and-so, a proud Bengal Sapper!" before receiving the traditional souvenir, a neatly wrapped Bengal Sapper tie.

But the dining-out ceremony was even more significant. A YO wasn't dined out upon leaving the Centre for another posting; he was dined out when he superannuated - when his career reached its final sunset. As the Centre Commandant, I took it upon myself to revive this tradition, writing to all superannuating Bengal Sapper officers and inviting them for their formal farewell at the Officers' Mess. It was a simple yet powerful way of showing respect and gratitude.

At Chandimandir, however, the ethos had undergone an unwarranted metamorphosis. As had been the case, officers posted to the Command HQ automatically became members of the Command Officers' Mess, and their dining-in was conducted collectively, given the sheer strength of officers. That was understandable. What was unfathomable was the capricious observance of the dining-out tradition. Every officer was a mess member, yet when they moved out, their dining-out and farewell ceremonies were conveniently reserved for a chosen few?

Every officer understands that with seniority in rank, some privileges come naturally. However, basic traditions, such as dining in/out and farewells, remain common for all. These are not about rank or stature but about the dignity of service and shared camaraderie.

The farewell tea party had also devolved into an almost comical spectacle. Intended as a gathering of camaraderie, it had become an awkward formality where the retiring officer, punctual and expectant, sat in isolation while the so-called attendees trickled in at their own leisurely pace, as if they were the stars of the show. I made it a point to attend these valedictory events, and it was disconcerting to witness the waning reverence for officers who were not in exalted ranks.

Then came the grand finale - the 'Buggy Ride'. The retiring officer, after his final cup of tea, would be ensconced in a horse-drawn carriage, with the military band playing a poignant farewell tune. If accompanied by his spouse, she would join him in this short symbolic ride before he would disembark and head home in his vehicle. A tradition of ineffable elegance, except that it had now become an arbitrary dispensation, dictated by the whims of a privileged few. More often than not, the retiring officer found himself in a solitary sojourn, with a perfunctory assembly going through the motions.

May 2022 heralded the retirement of a flag-rank officer. To my surprise, even he was denied a formal dining-out. The customary tea party invitation was extended as usual, but the officer, recognizing the hollowness of the ritual, declined outright. The HQ staff was momentarily discomfited, but as expected, the sands of time buried the moment in obscurity.

I mentioned this lacuna once to the COS at SEPTA. He listened with an impassive nod and responded, "I don't know if that was the case. I'll certainly look into it."

But in the Army, such assurances often disappear into the abyss of red tape, much like in higher HQ, where bureaucratic oblivion takes over!

Two months later, it was my turn. I was the senior most in service after the top man. The script remained unchanged - no invitation for a dining-out from the Officers' Mess. When the staff officer approached me, seeking a suitable date for my farewell tea, I merely smiled and said, "I'm not interested. I've seen enough of these charades."

He insisted, "Sir, you know there's the buggy ride. It's something to cherish all your life."

"What preposterous buggy ride?" I said. "I've had more than my fair share at Roorkee, with much more pomp and splendour!"

A personal call from the COS followed; an attempt at persuasion. "Sir, this isn't just for you; it's for all the officers... a tradition."

"Then uphold it for every officer, regardless of rank, in its most earnest way. That would truly honour the tradition. As for me, I've already made up my mind."

Reflecting on my tenure as Centre Commandant, I recalled our two exclusive buggies - one single-horse carriage driven by the Commandant himself, with a soldier seated behind; the other a grand two-horse carriage with a uniformed soldier at the reins, flanked by two ceremonial escorts and a backup staff car. Every Wednesday and Saturday, the Commandant left for his office in this regal fashion, an aesthetic spectacle that delighted onlookers. Civilians, young and old soldiers alike, waited eagerly to catch a glimpse of the buggy, something that gave the station a touch of nostalgia and grandeur.

This is neither a lament nor an indictment; it is an irony. The customs and traditions that once bonded officers as a single fraternity, irrespective of rank, are now fading. Progress and pragmatism are necessary, but the imbalance in privileges fragments the cadre. I bear no personal grievance. I have lived these traditions in their full glory. My earnest plea is for parity - a uniform observance of traditions that cultivate esprit de corps, dignity, and lifelong camaraderie. For when we relinquish traditions, we do not merely lose ceremonial rites; we forfeit the very soul of our institution.

कुछ शिकवे बने रहें तो बेहतर है,
चाशनी में डूबे रिश्ते मुख़्लिस नहीं होते।